Secret Women's Business

lingerie

confessions from the change rooms

A Lingerie Memoir

Pauline Kramer-Saxon

Secret Women's Business Lingerie
Confessions from the Change rooms: A Lingerie Memoir
© Pauline Kramer-Saxon 2020

ISBN: 978-1-922354-31-0 (paperback)

Edited by Kim's Net Solutions.
Published in Australia by Pauline Kramer-Saxon and InHouse Publishing.
www.secretwomensbusinesslingerie.com
www.inhousepublishing.com.au

Printed in Australia by InHouse Print & Design.

With all my love and affection
I dedicate this book to ...

My Mum: Lillian

My Dads: Tommy and Tommy

My wonderful, loving and particularly
gorgeous husband: Peter

And to all the lingerie loving ladies and
lads with fascinating tales to tell!

Contents

Chapter 1

Mum's shop

Mum was naïve.

Although a sophisticated woman in so many ways, there were many aspects of sexual and fetishist behaviour that she knew nothing about, and had no intention of ever discovering. If she didn't know about it or discuss it, then it didn't exist. And that was all right by her. She pretended to be a "sophisticated woman of the world," but she was privately shocked by anything out of the norm—and her norm came in a very small box. If she hadn't seen it growing up in London's East End, then it shouldn't exist.

Any behaviour that she didn't approve of would be mispronounced on purpose—as if saying it badly meant that it wasn't real. She took a great deal of time to pronounce each syllable as well— "HO-MO-SECK-SYOU-WAL" and "LES-SPI-YAN"— or, if she were in a rush, it would be "one of those" accompanied by a little flick of her wrist. And she would never look you in the eyes as she said it. Perhaps she thought that people would think that those words could never come out of her mouth if she didn't make eye contact. She couldn't even bring herself to say "blow job" in case someone thought that she might ever indulge in such behaviour.

So, when an exhibitionistic cross-dresser walked into her shop, she had no idea what to do.

Sydney in the early 1980s was still quite a conservative town. Men were men and women were little ladies. The corporate world was extremely macho; the best that a woman could hope for was office manager, maybe—general manager was unheard of. A secretary might work after getting married, but once she had children, her career was over. Women were welcome to start small businesses but couldn't get a credit card unless a man signed off on it. The gay community was very much in the closet: homosexuality was still a crime and the Gay and Lesbian Mardi Gras was only two years old, more of a protest parade than a celebration of sexual diversity. I had an openly gay piano teacher, but that was the only person in our circles who was not hiding his true self. No-one really minded, as he was "artistic". If there was anyone else, then we never knew. I think Mum was quietly pleased that he was gay because at fifteen I was quite well developed. I would go to his flat in the seedy part of Kings Cross's red-light district for my lessons, and hang out with him afterwards to talk about music and listen to him play. She knew I would be safe with him. I never told her about all the times I was accosted at the bus stop on the way home by men who thought my ample bust in a grey, box-pleat school uniform was a costume, and that they could rent me by the hour. I could have made a fortune!

My parents had divorced after my father left the family for a woman fifteen years younger than him. With Mum pushed out in the settlement, the divorce also meant the beginning of the end of my parents' lingerie and swimwear factory, and it never quite reached its former glory again.

It was a nasty and bitter battle with no pulled punches; my father installed his mistress in the business as a designer, leaving poor Mum humiliated, without employment and with two headstrong teenage daughters to raise.

However, with a great amount of courage and fortitude, Mum managed to pull herself together. She opened a lingerie store in the heart of Sydney's business district near a train station. She was also introduced to a new man who had a very strong physical resemblance to my father. Ironically, not only was he also Hungarian, but his name was the same as well. However, that was where the similarities ended. An architect, he was a kind and gentle man who dedicated himself to my mother's welfare and treated her like a queen. He indulged her every whim and mood—and still does to this day.

Business was quite good in the shop. It was stocked with a full range of the local brands—lots of basic bra sets with matching camisoles and slips, as well as sleepwear and elegant peignoir sets. It was the fashion then for young ladies, in anticipation of getting married, to collect lingerie for their "hope chest". A honeymoon was a honeymoon then; young brides would have a collection of lingerie, usually a white corset and stockings for the wedding night and then softer and more comfortable but still sexy sets for the rest of the honeymoon. What most brides didn't realise, of course, was that after the excitement of the wedding ceremony and reception, both she and her groom would be exhausted—so much so they would often just fall into bed and sleep! There was also a small section of the store set aside for some sexier garments—sheer teddies, babydolls, tie-side panties and bras which closed with a ribbon in the front. There were even some crotchless knickers and peek-a-boo bras.

Lingerie in the early 1980s was a simpler affair than it is today: it was something to be worn *under* your clothes; bra straps were never to be seen. Breast size was also much smaller than it is today. The average bra size was 12B, and DDs were almost unheard of. Breast implants were uncommon, and women seemed to be more content with their size, as padded bras were not a significant part of the range. Madonna had not yet burst on the scene wearing underwear as outerwear, and we had just come out of the "burn the bra" era. Women were wearing a lot of seam-free, moulded-cup bras in case someone might see a hint of lace—which was frowned upon, especially for any woman working in the business district. Dress codes meant that women couldn't wear trousers, and no-one would dare turn up to work without pantyhose on—even on the hottest of Sydney days. The sexier garments were very tame by today's standards and quite hard to come by. Often the only thing that differentiated them from the regular underwear was that they were made from the sheerest of fabrics.

It had been a long week and Mum was looking forward to the weekend. Friday was slow, so when a tall, slender, well-dressed gentleman walked in near closing time, she was pleased. Men are usually fabulous customers—they buy anything you show them and don't worry too much about price. Still, in the 1980s most Australian men wouldn't have been caught dead in a lingerie shop; unless they'd lost a bet. It just wasn't what a "real bloke" did. However, there were a few courageous trailblazers brave enough to enter the secret realm of ladies' undergarments. Most had no idea of size and would hold out their palms to show how big their wives' breasts were. If they held their hands palms up, you knew she was well endowed.

"Can I help you with anything?" my mum asked.

"No, thank you, I would just like to browse." He was softly spoken and seemed a little shy, not wanting to meet Mum's eyes.

So Mum returned behind the counter. She thought she would let him look for a bit.

He started to work his way through all the racks, making sure that he didn't miss anything. He made his way towards the sexy stuff and started to pull out garments, hanging them over his arm.

Before long he had a collection of about eight pieces, all sheer: teddies, babydolls, cami-knickers, suspender-camis. He looked at Mum and asked where the change-room was. Before she could even think about what he had asked, she pointed and off he went. She didn't know what to do! This wasn't a situation she had ever encountered before, and she wasn't at all prepared.

She could hear items being taken from their hangers, and the rustling of clothes being removed. After about ten minutes, he threw open the curtains and strutted three steps out of the change room, wearing nothing but the sheerest of red tie-side panties and a matching halter top with a big bow between the cups. It was designed for someone much shorter and nothing was left to the imagination as he raised his arms high in the air, thrust his hips towards Mum and adopted a high-pitched, lispy voice: "Tho, honey? How do you think thith lookth?"

Mum didn't know where to look, but as a well-brought up woman of her times she knew that if a man asked you a direct question, it was rude not to answer. "Uh … ummm … errrhhhhh … very nice," was all she could think to say, trying to avert her eyes from the very squashed bits trying to burst out of the knickers.

He smiled, pirouetted very slowly to give her a good view of his bottom as well, wiggled his hips and sashayed back into the change room, closing the curtains behind him with a flourish. He stayed there for at least another twenty minutes. Poor mum was beside herself, not knowing what the proper thing was to do under the circumstances. Asking him if he needed any help with the sizes didn't seem quite appropriate. Nor did asking him if he'd like to see anything in a different colour.

She was conflicted. On the one hand, she wanted a sale, but on the other, she wanted him out of the shop. She didn't feel that she was in any physical danger—or moral danger, for that matter. It did occur to her that when she closed her eyes that night she would be stuck with that image; how would she ever sleep again? How would she explain her insomnia to her husband? How could she even form the words in her mind to make sentences to explain what had happened?

The man remained in the change room for an inordinate amount of time before finally emerging fully clothed in his business suit. He closed the curtain behind him, walked up to the counter, dropped everything he had tried on in a big jumbled heap on the table and, without a word, walked out of the shop.

Mum sat there for a few minutes staring at the pile of lingerie, loath to touch any of it after it had been tried on by this … this… She didn't know what to call him, but in her mind, it was filthy and perverted. She was paralysed by indecision. What did she do now? She had to do something, but what?

Finally, she got up and went over to the change room to make sure there was nothing he had forgotten to bring out. She opened the curtains, looked inside and saw that the mirrors seemed very dirty. How could that be? She was sure that she had cleaned them that morning. She took a closer look and then nearly threw up; he had wiped semen all over the full-length mirrors. So that was what he'd been doing in there for so long.

She backed out of the change room in horror. "*Oy a bruch! Oy gevalt!*" she thought in a panic. She always reverted to her childhood Yiddish when in a bind. It seemed so much more expressive and appropriate. "Give me a break! Woe is me!" There were no other words that would do!

She sat down behind the counter for a few minutes till her composure returned. My mother was not one to let things get on top of her for too long. Sanity and commercial requirements overtook her need to lose her lunch, and she realised that a proper, "normal" customer could walk in at any moment—and how would she explain the mirror stains?

Mum replaced her usual "BACK IN TEN MINUTES" sign with a hand-written "BACK IN 30 MINUTES" sign and headed to the convenience store to pick up appropriate cleaning supplies. She came back with a thick plastic garbage bag and heavy-duty rubber gloves. The pile of lingerie went into the bag, as did the hangers they came with, and then she cleaned the mirrors, disinfecting them with Dettol and then polishing them with Windex. Even the curtains were removed for laundering. She wiped down the walls around the mirrors and vacuumed the carpet. She sprayed every possible surface in that change room with the strongest anti-bacterial disinfectant and then saturated the carpet with it.

Not long after this incident, I started to help out in the shop. I needed to supplement my babysitting money to help pay for my piano lessons. Before I started Mum sat me down and told me about what happened on this fateful day. She felt that if I was working there, I needed to know what might happen and be prepared. I was full of questions—fascinated by the naughtiness of it all and her reaction intrigued me. She was obviously embarrassed about having to describe what happened, turning a deep shade of pink as she answered all my questions but unable to look me in the eyes. She wouldn't utter the word "semen" but labelled it "his filth". After a while my incessant questions (I was secretly delighted by the salaciousness of it all and wanted to know every single detail. I knew it would make a great story for my school buddies and I couldn't wait to tell them!) upset her and she changed the subject.

After that, Mum eyed every man who walked into the shop with suspicion. It became The Rule—no man, without exception, was allowed to try on anything. EVER! EVER! EVER!

Mum is now in her late seventies. She comes into the shop once a week for a gossip and to see the new stock. She still looks spectacular; red hair and fair, unlined skin. She'd never think to leave the house without lipstick and earrings and is always dressed beautifully. A real lady. When I get to her age, I hope I look as good as she does. Once, I asked her what she remembered about the incident and all she could say was "Why are you asking me about this? I prefer not to remember horrible things," and then changed the subject.

Chapter 2

It was love at first sight

It was love at first sight. Heidi was petite, with large brown eyes and dark, curly hair that fell to her shoulders. He knew the moment he saw her that he would love her till the day he died. He was only fifteen years old, but surviving the war had made a man of him. He knew what he wanted—and he wanted her.

Budapest under Russian occupation was a terrible place. My paternal grandparents, Ernst and Margaret, lost almost every member of their large extended family in the Holocaust. They also lost their eldest son Dezso, my father's big brother. In the aftermath of the war they were trying to find a way to overcome the tragedy and make a future for themselves. Opa and Onya ("Dad" and "Mum" in Hungarian, but it became our name for them) had tried to resume their pre-war lives and started manufacturing lingerie again under their old company name—*Margit Melltarto* (Margaret Bras)—but communist Budapest was not the same as 1930s Budapest. Try as they might, it was impossible to get fabrics, sewing machines or even qualified staff. There were plenty of women who would have bought anything that they made—if they only had the money. There wasn't much of it around.

At that time the Russians were taking men randomly off the streets to send back to the mother country as labourers; Opa had already been taken twice. He managed to escape both times, and he and Onya knew they had to leave before it happened again. A distant cousin lived in Australia, and they somehow managed to arrange visas—but they had no exit papers. The only way out was to escape; which they did in the middle of the night, hidden in a boat that floated down the Danube. It cost them just about every penny they had, and they had to leave everything behind, including their passports. But then, in March 1949, after a perilous three-month journey that took them through Czechoslovakia and Bratislava, they finally arrived at a displaced persons camp in Vienna—not as refugees, because they had visas to Australia, but rather as proud "stateless people".

The camp was full of people who, just like them, were fleeing war and tyranny—all hoping to find a better life elsewhere. They had come from all over Europe but tended to group together by language and religion. The Hungarian Jews set up youth groups and schools, and this was where my father met Heidi, his first love. Both were young survivors, with uncertain futures and limited time together. Dad knew he would be coming to Australia, but Heidi had no idea where her family would end up. There was talk of going to Israel; even though the country had only recently been established and survived the War of Independence (First Arab-Is-raeli War). Being Orthodox, it seemed a good place for them to go, they wanted to be somewhere Jews could be free to live their lives without fear.

Heidi's parents never approved of my father. They wanted a religious boy for their daughter. As my father's family was completely secular, he would never be good enough. They tried desperately to stop the relationship, so the young couple had to meet in secret. When representatives from Israel came to the camp to help organise those who wanted to make *Aliyah* (literally, "going up", but the word is used for anyone immigrating to Israel), my father and Heidi were spotted together at one of the meetings, which petrified Onya and Opa. They had lost one son to the Nazis and didn't want to lose another to a country that was just recovering from its own war and had, as far as they were concerned, an uncertain future. As it turned out, fate intervened as after nine months my father and Heidi were torn apart. Passage to Australia was arranged; my father and his parents were off. There were no forwarding addresses; Heidi and my father said goodbye with the knowledge that they might never meet again.

After a long sea journey, my father and his parents arrived in Australia in early 1950. Life was good. They were free; free to walk the streets, free to associate with anyone they wanted, and free to start up their business again. They settled in Sydney and found a small house in Summer Hill where they started to make lingerie again, this time under the brand name VANITY. Opa made the patterns using Kellogg's cornflakes cereal boxes for paper, and Onya cut all the fabrics on the dining table. They invested in a sewing machine, but all the bows and ribbons were finished by hand. Australian lingerie at this time was quite simple; the European flair that they brought to the designs made their styles popular at Paddy's Market, where they ran a stall.

Their success led them to decide to sell to boutiques as well. Opa would carry all the samples around in an old cardboard suitcase, going from shop to shop to sell his wares. He was tall, distinguished and had a strong Hungarian accent that made him sound exotic to the local Australian shopkeepers. An old ear infection had left Opa nearly deaf, but he would say, "My English is not goot and I am hard of hearing, but if you give me an order, zat I vill hear!" And the product was good, so the orders came flying in.

With business booming, they employed two sisters, Greek girls called Rosa and Maria, who stayed and worked with my family for over twenty years. Dad was enrolled in high school, but after one year he decided that there was nothing more they could teach him; he managed to convince his parents that he should travel around New South Wales and sell their lingerie instead. Opa and Onya wanted him to stay in school and get an education, but once my father got an idea in his head, there was no talking him out of it—so off he went. He was spectacularly successful and after one month came back with enough orders to fund the purchase of a brand-new car!

The Hungarian community was small in number but had spread out across Australia. News travelled fast between them, and it came as a huge shock to my father to hear that Heidi was in Melbourne. He had never forgotten his first love, and even though it had been five years since he'd last seen her, he knew he had to get to her. He convinced his parents that the time had come to expand their business some more. He loaded up the car with samples and drove to Melbourne—a distance of 600 miles and at least two days of driving on the old Hume Highway. He found out where she lived and went straight over to see her. After the initial shock of finding him on their doorstep, her family let him in. However, the news was not good; she was engaged to a Polish boy. Her parents approved of her fiancé completely, as he was from a good Orthodox family. They told my father he should leave things in the past and move on.

Dad was devastated. The more he couldn't have her, the more he wanted her. She became an obsession. And with these thoughts in his head, he decided that the only way to deal with it was to become a playboy. Gambling, women, fancy clothes and cars became his religion.

Populate or perish

Australia needed people to help build the country. After World War II there was an influx of refugees from Europe, but in order to make sure that the population was balanced, British immigrants were also encouraged to come. To facilitate their journey, assisted passage was offered, and that was how my mother came to Australia. Her oldest sister and husband had arrived in 1951; Mum came to join them two years later at the age of nineteen. She was a Ten Pound Pom, thrilled to escape the drudgery of post-war London for the opportunities that Australia could provide. As she left, her mother handed her a couple of diamonds that had belonged to her Russian grandmother—she thought she would never see her daughter again and wanted to send her off with something precious.

Leaving her parents and two other sisters was difficult, but at the end of the six-week sea journey (during most of which she was horribly seasick), my mother knew that her skills as a typist would guarantee her a job. Within a week of arriving in Melbourne and moving into a small room at her eldest sister's house, she had a job and was finding her way. The city suited Mum just fine; there was plenty of work and plenty of places to go, although it was way too hot for her fair English skin—after her first severe case of sunburn, she never went to a beach again. A year later, her parents and another sister also became Ten Pound Poms, and the family was just about complete. However, one sister remained in London with her husband and son. Australia wasn't for everyone.

Most of the Jews in Melbourne had come from Poland, a community that had also been devastated by the Holocaust. Mum's middle sister met a sweet man, Yoseleh, who had passed through five concentration camps until finally being freed from Buchenwald. He had lost every single member of his family. He was weighed down by his losses and the importance of carrying forward the Jewish people, and with that in mind he introduced Mum to a friend of his, Izzy—also a survivor, but from a different camp, Auschwitz.

Izzy was Mum's first boyfriend; as such, she accepted everything about him, including his somewhat strange behaviour. The sudden angry outbursts and faraway looks seemed normal to her, as she knew no better. Unusual behaviour was not really all that "unusual"; growing up during the Blitz in London, she had encountered many men who had seen too much and whose expressions were often haunted. Her own home had been destroyed during an air-raid when she was nine years old, so trauma and loss were ingrained into her psyche. Survivors and their quirks were ordinary to her and everyone else she knew. Izzy was kind and soft-spoken; he treated her well. He never shouted at her even though he could be short-tempered with others, and that was all that mattered.

Because of this, Mum accepted his proposal within only a few months of their meeting, but it soon became apparent that all was not right. The stress of the engagement party and everyone's expectations took their toll, and Izzy began to withdraw into himself. After a long and difficult family discussion, my mother realised that he was way too damaged from his wartime experiences to ever make a good husband or father—and so she broke it off. They had a painful meeting, sitting together to organise the return of all the engagement gifts, and then a few days later he turned on the gas oven and placed his head inside. It was only that someone noticed the gas gauge spinning wildly that he was saved.

Guilt and relief were all my mother felt. Guilt that perhaps she caused him to attempt to take his life, even though she understood that the horrors of Auschwitz had never left him, and relief because she realised that the decision to break off the engagement had been the right one. She did not have the emotional capacity to deal with his pain. When telling me this story, Mum was also comforted by the fact that soon after their engagement ended Izzy met another lady; they married quickly and had children. "All's well that ends well," she said pragmatically.

Six months had passed, and the time had come for Mum to go out dating again. Her sisters wanted her to move on from Izzy and find someone so they could all go out on dates together, rather than worry about her being alone. After all, she was twenty-one now, and there were lots of eligible Jewish men around. Jewish singles house parties were a monthly event in Melbourne, advertised in the local Jewish newspaper, and were always very well attended. Members of the community were happy to donate their homes for these parties to offer a safe and intimate place for young Jewish people to meet. There was one planned for the coming Saturday night, and Mum's eldest sister and brother-in-law said they would go with her so she wouldn't have to walk in alone.

By the time they arrived, the party was in full swing—the record player was fired up, couples were dancing and there was even a roulette table operating in the back room. Mum was chatting to her sister, hoping that someone would come over and ask her to dance—she had been to the hairdresser, was wearing her best dress and wanted to be noticed—when her brother-in-law called them over. He wanted them to check out a fellow at the roulette table who had just lost twenty-five pounds—a fortune at the time—and was writing out a cheque to cover his losses.

Mum walked into the room just as my dad finished signing the check with a flourish. He looked up and surveyed the room, making sure that everyone could see how much he didn't care— and spotted Mum. He walked over to her, handed her a lolly—a Pez—and introduced himself, and then said, "You're fat". Who knew that such a pick-up line would be a winner? They chatted for a while; he told her that the twenty-five pounds was the last of his money, but he didn't care.

They made a date for the following week. Dad picked her up and drove her to a hall where they sat in the car outside, making no move to get out. Mum was confused but said nothing, too naïve to know what to do. Finally, after about ten minutes, my father turned to her and said, "You see that hall over there? The woman I love is marrying someone else inside right now."

Eighteen months later, they married. I asked Mum once what she could possibly have been thinking. Any objective view of their situation would have indicated a disaster in the making. "We were both on the rebound and we were both young and silly," was all she would say. None of her family approved of Dad, and when she travelled to Sydney to meet Opa and Onya, the "favour" was returned. My grandmother was furious with her son. How dare he bring home a girl who didn't speak Hungarian? A match made in hell. They even hired a private detective in London to check out that Mum's family were who they said they were.

Mum told me that the first time she walked into their house, Onya was sewing bows on to the legs of suspender belts and Opa was hand-sewing concentric circles of peach satin for a bullet bra. However, he was leaving the centre of the bra open so that the nipples would stick out. She was scandalised!

Against both of their parents' wishes, they insisted on marrying and had a lavish wedding in Melbourne before moving to Sydney. Onya gave my mum the best wedding present she could think of; a cardboard-box full of patterns cut out of Kellogg's cornflake boxes. "See vat you can do vid dis," she said to Mum. I'm sure she thought that Mum would fail, giving her another reason to disapprove of her new daughter-in-law.

Poor Mum—she had no idea what she had got herself into. However, the girl who'd left home at nineteen to travel halfway around the world by herself was not going to be scared off by a few bits of paper. She sat for hours staring at the cardboard patterns, trying to figure out how they all went together. The only writing on each piece of cardboard was the style name and size, and that was it. It was a like a jigsaw puzzle. But she was smart and had a good eye, and after a while it all began to make sense. Sensing her talent, Opa and Onya stepped back from the business and let Dad and Mum take over. She became the designer in the family business, creating her own patterns and updating the styles to reflect her taste. She added laces and embroideries and then began to branch out into making swimwear as well. There was one bikini that she designed that had over thirty-six pieces just in the top. Thirty-six pieces! Another style had forty-two daisies sewn over the bust and featured on the cover of a popular fashion magazine.

My mother's parents were brought up from Melbourne to help in the business, and they ran stalls at the markets on weekends. They also helped with looking after my sister and me. It was most unusual at that time for a mother to work full-time, and the help was greatly appreciated. The two sets of grandparents had little in common but were intent on helping their children—and they all doted on their grandchildren. Opa's only regret was that he was hard of hearing and couldn't hear the most beautiful sound in the world—the laughter of his granddaughters. Mum's mum loved selling in the markets. She would also go into the department stores which stocked Mum's styles and rearrange the racks to place her bikinis at the front, to make sure they were seen first. If ever she was challenged on this (the stores had their own merchandisers and did not appreciate her meddling), she would just laugh and say that these ones were much prettier—and then scurry away.

Dad dealt with the sales and the day to day running of the business, while Mum earned the grudging respect of my grand-parents through her sheer hard work and talent—and the fact that she also managed to produce two daughters. After a while, they seemed to stop worrying about the fact that she couldn't speak Hungarian and cared more about how they could spend more time with the grandchildren.

Onya died in 1967; Opa died four weeks later of a broken heart. Mum and Dad continued to build up the business until they had a couple of factories and employed over fifty people. But their marriage, not surprisingly, did not last. In the mid-1970s, they went through a nasty and bitter divorce, which meant the end of the business. Mum decided to open up a lingerie shop. Dad tried numerous and varied businesses, but none of them worked as successfully as when he had partnered with Mum. He turned his attention to dating many women and put all his efforts into becoming the playboy he'd always wanted to be.

Sydney, June 1990

Dad was dying. He had a horrible rare disease that kept all the professors at the hospital fascinated until they realised that there was no cure, and then they went on to more interesting cases. He was fifty-four, and it was a tragedy to see such a vibrant, strong man reduced to skin and bones within just one year of his diagnosis. He was in constant pain and was hooked up to a morphine drip to dull his senses. I sat with him for hours every day, just watching and talking to him but getting very little response. Old family friends would come to visit and walk away shaking their heads. "What a shame," they would say sadly. "Such a nice man." Dad hardly said anything but every now and then he would squeeze my hand.

The day before he finally slipped into a coma, he opened his eyes and seemed to look through me as he started to talk.

"She was so beautiful," he said in a very weak, raspy voice. "I will always love her."

"Who was so beautiful, Dad?" A silly part of me hoped that he would say my mum.

"Heidi—who else? She was so beautiful, and I wanted to marry her." He closed his eyes and seemed to drift away.

A few weeks after he died, I was going through some of his things when I found a leather satchel. Inside were unopened letters, ones he posted to her but that were marked "return to sender", and old black and white photographs of a dark-eyed beauty. They looked as if they had been held many times; they were rough around the edges from constant handling.

It was love at last sight, too.

Chapter 3

The secret of Secret Women's Business

You should be a lawyer!

Not "What do you want to be when you grow up" but "You should be a lawyer". Both of my parents thought so. I liked to argue the point, and my point was always different to theirs. I couldn't help it. Being contrarian was in my nature. And as far as I was concerned, I was always right—and I could prove it if only they opened their minds and listened. I could have also gone in for Talmudic scholar, but what kind of a profession is that for a nice Jewish girl?

Most arguments ended with them saying "Because I said so" as they had run out of answers. There was not much I could do about it because they were the boss of me, but I could tell they enjoyed the encounters. And if logic didn't work, then humour was a good alternative, and if *that* failed, it was very hard to refuse a dimpled, pigtailed, freckle-head with a mean pout!

In truth, though, they didn't understand me. I was fascinated by the arts. Visual—music—verbal. The rigours of following rules bored me. I never used recipes and cooked by sight and smell. Suffice to say, baking was a disaster! Knitting patterns were not for me, either. However, if I stared at a ball of yarn long enough, a finished garment would come into my head and I'd be off. Certainly, I made some major mistakes, but I also created some masterpieces. And history ... how I loved it. Stories of any sort entranced me, and there weren't enough hours in the day to read all the books I wanted to read. I'd practise the piano for hours every day and discovered heaven in a ten-inch vinyl recording of Gershwin's *Rhapsody in Blue*. Even having to turn it over halfway through didn't deter me. I listened to it over and over again.

More than that, *more than anything*, people and their stories fascinated me. And from a young age, friends and strangers talked to me. I must have one of those faces of a good listener. Whatever it is that makes people open up to me, I am always honoured that they shared their lives with me.

When I graduated high school, I received a scholarship to study at the Hebrew University in Jerusalem. After my psychometric testing results were tabulated, I could choose to study anything I wanted, except for medicine and psychology, neither of which appealed to me anyway. I chose teaching. It's such a noble profession, and I've had a number of inspiring teachers who changed my life. I wanted to be one of them.

After about three weeks of studies, I was on my way home from a day's classes, sitting on a bus packed with a rambunctious rabble of teenage boys. Rude and foul-mouthed, they were so annoying to everyone on the bus that I wanted to smack them. As an aspiring teacher I knew this would be an unacceptable way of imposing discipline and maintaining order. Yet I did not have the words or possess the skills to make them listen. And if I couldn't get a group of boisterous kids on a bus to settle down, what hope did I have of controlling a classroom?

If you mess up as a teacher, you can ruin kids' lives. After considerable soul searching, I concluded that I wasn't prepared to take on that kind of responsibility. It's way too important a job to screw up. So, teaching was out.

After some creative self-analysis, I decided that the perfect course of study for me in Israel would be archaeology. How fascinating it would be! In that part of the world, one can dig down almost anywhere and find a rich vein of ancient treasures—coins, pottery, parchments—proof that this or that legend actually happened. This idea came to me a full two years before Indiana Jones became the cool new face of archaeology in Spielberg's *Raiders of the Lost Ark*.

Sadly, my dream of discovery lasted just one week of lectures before I discovered that archaeology was not for me. When you're an archaeologist, you go on digs. All the digs in Israel are from March through October, in the heat … the hot, Lawrence Of Arabia heat … the skin-burning, horrendous, hot-heat that makes my fair, freckled skin sizzle like meat on a spit and blinds my pale eyes. I'd be lucky to last fifteen minutes in those conditions, let alone the rest of my working life. I'd end up looking like a boiled lobster, and we all know that that is not a good look for a nice Jewish girl.

Having struck out twice in search for a meaningful career, I thought and thought and then I thought some more. Eventually I realised that I should study what actually interested me: art history and musicology. I also did a minor in theatre studies. I loved every minute of it. And it qualified me to do absolutely nothing. Nothing at all. BUT—and this is the most important part—I could bullshit about anything and everything! I was a natural.

Seriously, though, studying art, music and theatre, without much hope it would lead to paid employment, was one of the best decisions I've ever made. It taught me to look beyond what's obvious and to listen beyond what people are saying. I could easily find beauty in everyone and everything. Ugly is as ugly does.

Every woman is beautiful—especially when she smiles. It made me understand that we all have a story; if you learn to observe facial expressions and respond to people, you'll find they want to open up and tell you all about themselves, their thoughts, dreams, fears and innermost feelings. Their stories are often fascinating and inspiring; they'll enrich your life just by hearing them.

I came back to Sydney after my marriage broke up. We had met on the first day of uni. He walked into the classroom, tall with a mop of unruly curls, and I elbowed my friend and whispered, "I quite like the look of him—I think I'll have him!" We married too young. It happens. You grow up and change and then realise that you want different things than you thought you wanted at eighteen. There was no anger or bitterness in the breakup, just sadness that it didn't work out. On reflection, I felt the need to have my family close, so I came back to Australia.

I moved back to my mum's home and slept in my sister's old bedroom, as mine was being used for storage. It felt like I had never left home, except I woke up on the other side of the house and was now thirty years old, starting again with nothing. No marriage, no job, no real savings and no house of my own—I had left it all to the ex because I was exhausted and had no appetite for potential acrimony over settlement negotiations. Everything that I had worked towards over the past decade to become a self-supporting, independent adult had gone. Disappeared. It was over. That part of my life was gone forever.

I didn't know what to do with myself; I felt completely lost and out of kilter. After a couple of months of moping aimlessly about, Mum suggested that I come to her shop and sit with her for a bit. I had no real plans that day, or any other for that matter, so I figured why not?

She was no fool my mother, no fool at all. I got in there and started poking around the shop and rearranging things—

and before you could say, "would you like to see the matching G-string," I had found my forte. I had a knack for looking at a customer and knowing her size and which style would suit her figure best. Mum spent time explaining many of the design features and manufacturing processes that went into each garment as well as the way different fabrics behaved and how they could be applied to different parts of a garment. Before too long, I developed an inherent understanding of lingerie in all its forms, as well as women in all of theirs.

Every customer was like a fascinating enigma, each with their own particular wants and needs. I could normally solve them easily with just a few simple questions, but every now and then, it became more intriguing. Sometimes a question would elicit an unexpected response and it became not just about lingerie—the first thing they would put on and the last thing they take off—but about their lives.

I noticed Maria staring at the display window near the entrance to the shop. She looked conflicted. Taking the final step through the door seemed too much of a leap for her. Finally, she summoned up the courage and came in. She took a few steps into the shop and looked around. She seemed overwhelmed by all the bras and briefs on the racks, so I asked if I could help her find something. She looked at me blankly for a moment, took a deep breath and let it out slowly. She took another one and then another.

"I've just been given the all clear," she said in a shaky voice. She looked me in the eyes. "The all clear," she repeated. "I'm all clear!"

She seemed to be in shock. And exhausted. The words she wanted so desperately to hear had finally been spoken; now she needed to absorb them into her core. The more she said them herself, and said them out loud, the more real they became.

"That's wonderful!" I moved towards her and gave her a hug. She let me put my arms around her and she put her head on my shoulder and sobbed, great heaving sobs of relief. It may have been the first time she had exhaled properly since she'd received her initial diagnosis.

"Two years of hell. That's what I've had," Maria said. She was slowly finding her way back to sanity and regular breathing. "Colo-rectal cancer. Three operations till they found it all. Six months of chemo. I've gained all this weight from the meds. Hair loss. The waiting for results. The whole catastrophe. But I don't care. I don't care one bit. I just got the all clear. THE ALL CLEAR!" She shook her head in disbelief. For the last couple of years, the only happiness she'd felt had come from the absence of pain. Every waking moment and many dreaming ones had been filled with anxiety and fear. But that was all in the past now and she was pushing herself to move forward.

"I need a new bra," she told me. "My body has changed so much since all this began and nothing fits. I've been walking around in loose clothing for the last six months and I've been too scared to look in the mirror."

I led her to the change room and took a quick measurement. She had been a 14F before she got sick but now looked closer to an 18G. I asked her what colours she wanted—she just wanted something that was comfortable and a good fit. The colour didn't matter. She faced the wall, her back to the mirror, as she talked to me. It was obviously she was self-conscious and ashamed of her body since it had been so cruelly disfigured by her illness.

I wanted to give her the most vibrant bra I could, so she could focus on the colour rather than her body. I found a delicate lace balconette bra with beautiful lace detail on the strap in a bright cobalt blue. It had matching full briefs with lace inserts on the front and a keyhole feature on the back. I handed it to her through the closed curtains to give her time to try it on, catching a glimpse of her as I did; she still had her back to the mirror.

"Just let me know when you're ready and I can check the size for you," I said and left her to try it on in privacy.

After a few minutes, I heard a sharp intake of breath from the change room. I went over and asked if she was ready. When I opened the curtains, there she was, staring at her reflection in the mirror. The bra fit her well and so did the briefs. Her torso was covered in long red scars from her numerous operations, but she wasn't looking at those. She was smiling. It was apparent that this was the first time, in a long time, that Maria saw herself as something more than a collection of angry red scars. She wasn't seeing what was wrong—just what was right.

And there it was. That look in her eye. The joy … the pride in being a beautiful woman and not just a survivor. And in some small way, I helped her find it. I helped her feel better about herself.

That's why I love my shop.

Chapter 4

I found my perfect fit

I had been single for two years and I was feeling lonely. I sometimes envied those women I met who were divorced and angry—foolish, I know. But at least they had something to feed off. I felt no anger, just sadness; I missed the lost friendship.

In the days before rsvp.com.au the only real way to meet people was through Singles Parties—which I hated—or introductions. I had been set up on numerous blind dates; I could just hear everyone saying to all the eligible men they knew, "Oy, have I got a girl for you!" It was never about being suitable for each other. I was single; they were single. Thus: "Go! Meet! Who knows? Magic might just happen!"

Most dates were just a pleasant evening out; there was never a real spark with any of them. I just figured that men were intimidated by a buxom redhead with strong opinions—and if that were the case, then none of them were man enough for me. I think that a lot of those men were also confused about the business I was in. "Lingerie" seemed to have connotations they were unsure about.

The worst date I had was with a well-known lawyer who took me to a very expensive Japanese restaurant in Kings Cross, in the centre of Sydney's red-light district. The evening was quite pleasant; the conversation and the wine flowed, and for all intents and purposes I was enjoying myself.

UNTIL!

We were walking back to the car and he began to point out all the prostitutes he had slept with. I don't know if that was meant to impress me or excite me. I have no idea what his intention was, but the result was that I was repulsed. I can't imagine why he thought I might be amused or even turned on by such admissions. Maybe he didn't like me, and it was his way of giving me the kiss off; or maybe he thought that because I was in the lingerie business that I might be excited by his experience with women. Who knows?

I knew I was safe with him on the way home as he had been introduced to me by a colleague of his, and it would have done him no favours to behave inappropriately. However, I did sit as far away from him in the car as I could, and after a silent ride home, I bolted from the car with a quick "Thank you for dinner!" (Mum always taught me to say please and thank you, and I wasn't about to forget my manners, even if he had.) I just hoped he wouldn't try to escort me to my front door. As is the custom with blind dates, I reported what had happened back to the "matchmaker" who had set us up. He'd had no idea about this person's "other life" and apologised profusely. Many years later, I was sitting with a group of girlfriends and we were discussing bad dates. I mentioned this one, and when one of the girls asked what his name was, it turned out he was her father. She wasn't in the least surprised.

When I was growing up all of my school holidays were spent in my parent's factory. I helped out with every aspect of the business, from cutting threads when the machinists had finished their work, to packing and checking orders and sealing boxes. There was always something to be done. In high school I used to help Mum out in her shop, so I knew how to fit bras already, and while I was living overseas, I managed fashion retail shops. I had a good eye for style and fit, and what I didn't know, Mum taught me. Going back to helping Mum in her shop, led to us working full-time together. It was a perfect fit for both of us.

The shop was humming along quite nicely, and we worked well together. The business was growing. We were in an arcade in the middle of the business district that led on to a busy train station in Sydney, and a lot of our clients were lawyers and financiers. The general need for most of our customers was for bras that took attention away from their breasts. It was hard enough for women to break through the glass ceiling in the 1990s to become executives in large companies, and the last thing they wanted was to be perceived as trading on their looks in any way. They wore dark-coloured business suits, just like their male co-workers, and nothing could be too fitted or accentuate their shape in any way. They might wear a colourful shirt under their jackets, but no button would remain undone.

Men expressed their personalities with elegant ties and perhaps a matching pocket handkerchief, women with strands of pearls. Minimiser bras were our best sellers while padded bras were not popular at all. Women wanted to shift attention away from their bustline as much as possible. However, as no-one would turn up to work in a skirt above their knees, stockings and suspender belts were also in demand. Not seamed stockings, of course, and definitely not fishnets—that would cause a riot in the office!

We also did a roaring trade in edible underwear and even had a sugar-free version for diabetics. Our male customers were very respectful; if anyone misbehaved in any way, it was very easy to find out where they worked and make a complaint. However, every now and then some sleaze would hang about outside the shop, peering through the window in the hope that the change room curtain would flap open and he'd catch a glimpse of some skin. Building security would be informed and they'd be sent on their way. The most disturbing thing that happened was when a man came in wearing business shirt attire with trousers that had pleats in the front. He asked if he could just browse and went from rack to rack. I let him be, as he obviously didn't want any help. After a while, I realised he was touching all the bras with one hand but the other was deep in his pocket and seemed to be rather busy. I told him to leave, or I'd call security.

Another inappropriate thing that would happen was that every school holiday we got bored teenage boys with barely broken voices making prank calls. As this was before the time of caller ID, there was nothing we could do about it. They always asked the same question—what colour underwear are you wearing—and then they'd crack up laughing. Harmless, but annoying. They might do it five times in a row, each time with a slight variation— "what size bra are you wearing", "can you wear a G-string backwards", "do you put your bra on first or your panties". All silly and juvenile. Unfortunately, even if you know it might be a prank call, you still have to answer the phone each time it rings in case it's a legitimate customer. No point in getting angry with them, as they'd just do it even more in the knowledge that they were pissing you off.

On this particular day, the phone rang and I picked it up. "Can I help you?"

"What colour knickers are you wearing?"

Okay—this one had a deep voice and was definitely a man, and there were no childish giggles in the background. I thought I would give him a chance to exit gracefully without me encouraging him and said, "I beg your pardon, I didn't hear what you said. Would you mind repeating that again?"

He hung up. Five minutes later the phone rang again, and it was the same voice.

"So, you didn't tell me what colour panties you're wearing."

"I'm sorry," I said, "but this is a terrible line—would you mind repeating that?"

Click. Someone obviously had too much time on his hands. I thought that would be it, but sure enough, ten minutes later the phone rang again. I was in the middle of helping someone into a corset and was telling her about the prank phone calls. One of the day-to-day hazards of working in the lingerie business. Mum took my place in the change room as I went to answer the phone.

"What colour panties are you wearing?" he asked again. "Maybe you don't want to tell me because you're not wearing any at all."

Okay then. If that's how you want to play it, I know how to fix you.

"Just one minute," I said into the phone. Then I called out in a loud voice so he could hear, "Mummy—there is a gentleman on the phone for you! He seems desperate to know if you are wearing any knickers and if so, what colour."

The lady Mum was helping into her corset burst out laughing. For some unknown reason, the line went dead!

It seemed like he got the hint, and we got on with serving customers. Then, about an hour later, the phone rang again.

"Hello?" It was that same voice. "Can I speak to Pauline, please?"

How did he know my name? That was weird.

"My name is David," he said. "I play tennis with your brother-in-law and he gave me your phone number. I was wondering if perhaps you would like to meet for a coffee."

You have got to be kidding me!

"David—I seem to recognise your voice from somewhere," I

said sweetly. "Was it you who called three times today to enquire about my underwear wearing habits?"

"Yes, that was me," he said. "I heard you have a good sense of humour."

Well, I've never been accused of not appreciating a good joke or a funny situation, but this was neither. The most generous interpretation was that he had extremely poor judgement and a terrible sense of humour. Either way, I did not want to have anything to do with him.

"David. Would you mind doing me a big favour? You know that piece of paper that has my phone number on it? Please tear it into tiny pieces and throw it away."

I called my brother-in-law immediately and told him what had happened. He was shocked. He'd thought David was a nice enough guy, but you just never know do you. I told him I was offended—David's behaviour was completely inappropriate. Had he thought I'd be impressed or turned on? How could anyone think that that was an okay opening to an introductory conversation? On top of everything else, it was also a place of business. What if Mum had answered the phone? My brother-in-law had no answers and apologised for my having to put up with such boorish behaviour.

The next day at lunch time, a man walked into the store bearing a huge bunch of flowers.

"Are you Pauline?" he asked, spotting me. "My name is David. I would like to apologise. I offended you. It wasn't my intention. I guess I just have a weird sense of humour." He held out the flowers. "Do you mind if we start again?"

A number of choice insults came to mind. I was seriously considering giving him a substantial piece of my mind. However, maturity has given me a certain amount of wisdom. There was nothing to be gained from it, and I figured he was embarrassed enough. I took the flowers and said I accepted the apology. That said, I really didn't think that there was any point in us going out since we were obviously very different people.

I dumped the flowers in the nearest bin as soon as he left. If nothing else, the experience was sure to make a good dinner conversation when I was next out with the girls.

A few months later, I was sitting at home on a Monday night. I was still living with my mum and my stepfather but was planning to move out soon. The Academy Awards were on TV and Billy Crystal was at his hilarious best. The phone rang in the middle of a particularly funny bit; I was going to let it ring out so that I could watch but decided to pick it up anyway.

"May I speak to Pauline, please. My name is Peter," the caller said, "and I have been given your number by a mutual friend."

Gosh—I remember thinking to myself. What a sexy deep voice he has. And polite too! Not like that other fool.

We started chatting, and before I knew it, a couple of hours had passed. We seemed to have a lot in common, and it turned out he had even been on blind dates with a number of my friends! I remembered being told about him by a girlfriend whose parents knew his parents. They'd thought about setting us up about six months earlier but decided it was a bad idea as I was a "bohemian" (HAHA!) and he was a businessman, so we probably weren't a good match!

He asked me what I was looking for in a man. I listed the things that were important to me:

1. Must be close to his family. I have a large extended family that I genuinely like, and anyone I am with would have to understand that. He came from a small family—just him and his folks—but they were very close. TICK.
2. Must enjoy food. I hate fussy eaters. They tend to be fussy about everything in their lives and spend too much time

looking for faults rather than enjoying life. "Stick with me," he said. "You'll never eat bad food or drink bad wine." TICK.

3. Must love dogs. If someone can't find pleasure in a fluffy puppy, they have no understanding of cute, and cute is the basis of fun. Easy. Another TICK.

4. Must love opera. This was more difficult. I love opera, and part of the joy is sharing it with someone else who enjoys it too. He said that he thought a tenor singing at full power was the epitome of masculinity. A BIG, GIANT TICK!

So I asked him what he was looking for.

"A busty redhead who owns a pub. But I'll settle for one who owns a lingerie shop."

I laughed. We arranged to meet the following evening. He was to pick me up at 7.00 pm.

That night, when Peter was picking me up, my mum and stepfather arrived home at the same time. They met up in the driveway. My stepfather Tommy took one look at him and said, "Hi there, Peter. How are your parents?" It turned out they'd been friends for many years, and he had known Peter since he was a little boy. We left for our date, and as they walked into the house, Tommy turned to my Mum and said "We'd better start preparing for a wedding. They'll get married!"

It was love at first sight. We went to an Italian restaurant and stared into each other's eyes over pasta. I was wearing my best cleavage; Pete did his best not to look, but he managed to sneak a few discreet peeks in, his eyes sparkling in anticipation! He had a very healthy attitude to women and lingerie. He explained that as far as he was concerned, lingerie was gift wrapping. I liked that. A lot! We were a perfect fit. I have a generous bust (to say the least!) and he had a bit of a paunch. When we hugged, it was like two perfectly matched pieces of a jigsaw puzzle fitting together.

We saw each other every day and after two weeks he proposed over tapas and sangria. I said yes, like it was the most normal of questions to which there was only one answer. Three weeks after we met, I moved in with him. We now live in a big terrace house with a fabulous red kitchen and a well-stocked wine cellar which is well guarded by two attack poodles. We travel the world to see opera and visit lingerie trade fairs. He seems to have gotten over the disappointment of me not owning a pub!

Chapter 5

Everything must match

Saturdays in the shop can be a madhouse. Normally, I can handle it by myself, but sometimes my niece, Natalie, comes in to lend a hand. I have to admit, the crazier it is, the more I love it—running from the change rooms to the racks to the till to the storeroom is a hoot. I thrive on the business, and it really is a lot of fun. The shop has been designed so that no-one can see anything from the street. Mum's shop had a design flaw where the change rooms were visible from the front window. We often had to shoo men away, or call security, as they would hang around in front of the shop in the hope of seeing a customer in a state of undress through a half-open change room curtain.

In my shop, the change rooms sometimes fill up, and the more adventurous ones will just try on their choices behind the racks. The shop can end up looking like a brothel, with half-naked women walking around in lingerie, admiring themselves in front of mirrors deliberating whether a push-up bra or a plunge would make their bust more alluring. If I notice that a gentleman has entered in the middle of the mayhem I will sing out "MAN IN STORE". Some will scurry back to the change rooms, but others will just parade around, half-dressed, displaying themselves in all their glory. Mostly the men look conflicted—they would love to stay and watch but don't quite know where to look without getting slapped. They just end up figuratively slapping themselves in the face and walk out—smiling, I might add!

This Saturday was no different. I was in my element running around and Natalie was taking money and hanging up the piles of discarded bras. Getting the perfect fit can take up to an hour and may mean trying on a dozen bras, so we can get into a mess very easily. In the middle of this mayhem, I noticed a new lady in the shop. Attractive, petite with long blonde hair and in her mid-thirties, she had large blue eyes and an upturned nose. She instantly reminded me of a Stepford Wife—pretty, slender and dressed in a very feminine manner, with every detail tidily in place. You could almost see her wearing an apron over a fully flounced skirt, a pink ribbon holding a high ponytail while she baked cupcakes—perfect in every way, but hiding an inner sadness. She looked like she was just going through the motions—looking but not seeing, touching but not feeling. She declined help but continued to browse.

Two weeks later she was back, but the store was much quieter that day, and Natalie wasn't working. She said that she had just lost a lot of weight and needed a fitting for new bras. I led her to the change room. I try to glean as much information as I can from my customers so I can understand where they are in their lives. As she was changing, she told me her name was Caroline. I asked why she had lost weight; she seemed to be quite fine-boned and didn't look like someone who needed to lose weight. Although she looked a little tired, her face didn't look like it belonged to someone who had recently lost a lot of weight.

"Stress," she told me. About thirty seconds later she added, "From a divorce". Her voice was brittle and rose in pitch as she spoke; it was obviously a very fragile time for her.

It seemed to me that she was only just managing to hold it together, so I turned the conversation back to what she was looking for. She was after something simple and basic in beige, like a T-shirt bra. I took a quick peek at her to gauge what size she needed. I have a very experienced and observant eye and can tell what size a woman needs just by looking. I am always right … except for when I'm wrong, and that doesn't happen very often!

I brought her a new style that had just been delivered. It was like a T-shirt bra, seam-free with a moulded cup, but instead of a flat stretch microfibre over the cup, it had moulded lace. It was a pretty ivory with pastel pink bows adorning the strap. All bras need some kind of adornment on them—either between the cups or where the straps are attached. Just a small bow or even a little button between the cups is all that's required. If there is no detailing at all, the bra just ends up looking cheap and unfinished. Some bras come with elaborate diamante drops or even long draping bows in bright colours.

Although it was a perfect fit, she felt that all she needed at this point was something plain and unattractive, as if her underwear choices should reflect her life.

"Can I offer my opinion?" I asked. Before she could respond, I continued, "It takes the same amount of time to put on something lovely as it does to put on something ugly, so why make a conscious choice for ugly?"

It had never occurred to Caroline that that was what she was doing—punishing herself with ugliness because she was sad. Women do this a lot. We punish ourselves with ugliness because we are sad or busy or even merely tired. Sometimes it's because we think that if no-one is looking at us, there's no point in wearing anything nice. And sometimes it's because we think we don't deserve anything better. No matter the reason, it's still self-punishment. I had one lovely lady who was brought in by her friends to get a new bra because what she was wearing not only fit poorly but also had a big hole in it. This particular woman told me that she couldn't have anything nice as she had five children. I asked her if she had four children, did that mean she could have something 20% nicer, but if she had six children it would have to be 15% uglier? When it was put to her like that … well, there really is no argument, is there!

I convinced Caroline to take the pretty bra and the matching panties, as well as another set in a pale shade of apricot with a diamond heart dangling between the cups and in the centre of the elastic on the matching briefs. She seemed pleased with her new acquisitions, and as I wrapped them in tissue paper, she thanked me for pushing her away from the concept of underwear as self-flagellation.

About three months later, Caroline came back looking for sleepwear. I asked her how she was going, as she was still obviously on edge. She said she was thinking of starting to socialise again. However, while her lingerie choices were pretty (I won't have anything unattractive in the shop), they were still conservative and utilitarian. Her purchases were more about just replacing old items rather than indulging herself with items that would bring her pleasure to wear. She also insisted on having cotton panties to wear with the nighties—a remnant from her convent school upbringing, she said, as the nuns frowned on any kind of nakedness, even when sleeping, and even now she would feel sinful if she didn't wear them.

She dropped off the radar again for a few months, but then the next time she appeared, I felt that there had been a change. Sure enough, she had started to see a new man—a stockbroker in his early forties. They had met through a mutual friend, and she told me there had been an instant attraction. He was tall, extremely handsome and sported a very well-groomed beard. He loved lingerie and had expressed a preference for long ivory sleepwear. He loved how feminine she was, and she glowed from the appreciative male attention. Her ex-husband had made her feel unattractive and inadequate as a woman, and this new man made her feel like she was getting back in touch with her femininity. She bought a simple ballerina-length silk chemise and matching robe. The next week she was back and reported he had loved it … and did I have anything else? This time we found a full-length, mushroom pink, bias-cut silk nightie with lace inserts that resembled styles from the 1930s. The silk draped perfectly over her petite figure, gently hugging and accentuating her curves, and the colour flattered her fair skin. She looked like she could have stepped out of a Katharine Hepburn movie—glamorous and strong, yet still quite vulnerable.

Two weeks later she was back again, and this time she seemed to have a better understanding of what he liked. We chose an ivory set: bra, bikini brief, suspender belt and stockings to match. It was all about ivory and soft fabrics and lace, she said. He had particular tastes, and lucky for him, she also liked the ultra-feminine look. The colour had started to come back to her face. She possessed an inner glow of joy, and the stress seemed to be a thing of the past. She proudly showed me a picture of the two of them at a party. He was tall and very handsome, with a full head of dark, wavy hair, and they were looking at each other with adoring eyes. It was very much a photo of two people in love! When she left, I watched her walk up the street with her new purchases. Her hips swung from side to side as her pleated skirt swirled around her with each step. She was the epitome of a woman in love.

She took to calling me every few weeks to see if there was something new for her, and I began to order individual pieces with her in mind—pretty and feminine things in pale colours. She would walk into the shop with a big smile on her face each time she knew there was something new. She said she had finally figured out what he liked: "He wants me to look like a virginal bride on her wedding night".

Well, that was easy enough to do. I found corsets and waspies in ivory, even a little chemise with a sheer mesh back and a peek-a-boo cutaway over the bust, some fantastic stockings with diamante and bow details, suspender belts and tie-side knickers. She drew the line at quarter cups—she felt that was just too raunchy and not bridal at all, but more for a honeymoon. A little risqué was fine, but it shouldn't be too overt. She was having the best time of her life. Her first husband had stopped looking at her years ago, and although she was very conservative by nature, she still wanted to be desired. This new man made her feel beautiful and sexy, for the first time in decades. Whenever something arrived for her, I would call her up, and when she realised it was me, she would start giggling into the phone in anticipation of what I had found for her.

One day Caroline walked into the shop and I sensed a change—if she had been happy before, she was now dripping with excitement. I thought maybe I should follow her around the shop with a bucket and mop! She waited till there was no one in the shop—she obviously had something very special to tell me. I thought that maybe he had proposed, and she needed something spectacular for the real wedding night. Whatever it was, she seemed ready to bust right out of her skin. She was radiant something; I couldn't quite tell what, but whatever it was, she couldn't wait to get it out.

"I know I can tell you anything," she said when we were alone, "and you won't judge."

Well, being in this business for so many years, of course there is nothing I haven't heard. There is plenty of stuff that I personally wouldn't do, but that's just me. I would never wear black and brown together (UGH!) or bungee jump, for that matter, but lots of people do, and good luck to them. That's their choice.

She took a deep breath and continued. "So, you know how he likes me to wear all the ivory bridal lingerie." Her voice seemed to crack with the anticipation of saying the words out loud.

"Yes," I said, nodding. She obviously was desperate to tell me something, but her mouth hadn't ever formulated the words, so she was taking her time.

"Well, it turns out that he likes to wear it, too." Her eyes glazed over for a moment as she savoured the words. "I can't talk to anyone about this but you. No-one would understand."

What a shock that must have been—a deep, dark secret confessed. I don't know how I would have reacted if that had been foisted on me.

"So," I said, "what did you say?"

"Oh, Pauline … What could I say? I love him. But you should know that if the sex was good before, it is INCREDIBLE now! We sit together in a candlelit room, both of us in silk peignoir sets and stockings and suspender belts … and WOW! It is the best that I have ever known."

"How did he tell you?" I asked. "I mean, you have got to be feeling very brave to share something like that. He must love you and trust you very much."

"We went out for dinner and then saw *La Bohème* at the Opera House. It was such a beautiful production! There was even a scene at the end of the first act, in the café, where the ballet corps were wearing corsets and stockings. When we came home we were sitting in the lounge drinking wine, and he told me how much he loved seeing me in my lingerie. Then he asked if I would like to see him model some, too. I was a bit surprised, but I said yes. I have to admit, it was just so exciting! I felt like I was entering a new world. In all honesty, he looked so masculine and handsome in his stockings and suspender belt. AND SO SEXY!" Her voice took on a breathless tone as she was speaking, as if she were reliving the moment. "He had tried to tell his first wife, but she couldn't cope," she explained. "She didn't want to know and anyway, she couldn't understand why he would want to go into competition with her! What a fool she was. I just love this man so much!"

She was so happy. Her face glowed and her eyes sparked, and I gave her a hug and told her how happy I was for her.

"What do you have in his size?" she asked. "He will need a size 16. I have his measurements here."

So, we picked out matching peignoir sets and suspender belts with matching ivory stockings-petite for her and extra-talls for him. I also found some elbow-length ivory satin stretch gloves and a couple of wrist-length lace gloves as well. They were planning a trip away and wanted to take a suitcase full of lingerie and nothing else. Finding matching bras was a little trickier, as the cup had to sit flush against the pectoral muscle or it would stand out, but the wire had to be wide. However, I managed to find a strapless bra that did the trick. As I wrapped everything in tissue, she told me that she has never been this happy in her whole life. Ever. She'd found the perfect man, and EVERYTHING about him was wonderful. She couldn't wait to show him all the beautiful things she bought.

However, she did also buy six pairs of plain beige cotton knickers so she wouldn't sleep naked. Those nuns were still whispering in her ear!

Postscript

Two years later they married in a beautiful church ceremony surrounded by all their family and friends. She wore a beautiful fitted full-length, ivory lace gown; it was high-necked, long-sleeved and skimmed her curves. Her hair was styled in a French twist, and the long, embroidered veil was sprinkled with diamonds. She carried an exquisite bouquet of cream roses. He wore an elegantly tailored black suit with an ivory shirt and a black and ivory tie. A cream rose was pinned to his lapel. And under their bridal finery they were both wearing identical ivory silk suspender belts and stockings. It was a perfect match.

Chapter 6

Weaponised wardrobe of mass destruction

I could hear them arguing from halfway up the street. The lunch crowds were returning to their offices.

"How could you do that to me?" she screamed at the top of her voice. "I have never been so embarrassed in my whole life!"

I went to the door so I could see what was happening. A pretty, petite woman in her mid-thirties, with straight blond hair falling to her waist, was staring daggers at a tall, handsome man wearing a well-tailored dark suit and tie. He was holding his hands in the air, palms up, looking completely perplexed.

"I don't understand what I've done wrong." He spoke in low tones, as if trying to appease her. "Why don't we go home and talk about it?"

"No. You go. Just leave me alone. I need to think."

Defeated, he turned and walked away, his shoulders slumped, his head bowed.

She didn't bother to turn to watch him leave; instead, she looked up to see all eyes on her. I backed away from the door, hoping she wouldn't notice that I'd been watching as well. Before I knew it, she had stormed into the shop and was angrily flicking through the racks.

I asked if she needed any assistance with sizes and she answered, "I suppose you heard".

"Everyone heard," I said with an apologetic smile. No use pretending otherwise. Since she'd brought it up, she obviously wanted to talk about it.

"I can't believe him," she said furiously. "After all the time we've been together, he goes and pulls a stunt like this. He called this morning and said he wanted to meet me for a special lunch."

I nodded encouragement but stayed quiet. She pulled a red bra from the rack and turned it over in her hand to check the size, but she was so filled with nervous energy that the bra held no real interest, and she put it clumsily back on the rack. It fell to the floor, taking a few others with it.

"Don't worry about that—everything falls down in here,' I said, bending over to pick them up and return them to the rack in no particular order.

"I normally have coffee and a sandwich at my desk, so I took a couple of hours off to meet him here. All was going fine till dessert arrived, and then he got down on one knee and pulled out the biggest diamond ring you've ever seen and proposed."

"Oh, how wonderful!" I gushed. I am a hopeless romantic. I cry at every wedding scene in movies. It's that moment when the groom turns around and sees his bride walking down the aisle towards him. It gets me every time. I even cry watching the video of my own wedding, even though I've seen it dozens of times.

"I couldn't believe it. In front of all those people! I told him to get up—he was embarrassing me. What was he thinking?"

"So, you said no?" I asked in surprise.

"No, I didn't," she answered, nervously pulling bras and briefs off the racks—choosing one while knocking three or four others to the floor. I followed behind her, picking items up and replacing them on the racks. She seemed oblivious to the mess she was making, and oblivious to me as well. She seemed to be thinking out loud, trying to justify her actions.

"I didn't know what to say. I don't know what I want—I just didn't want *that*. He's normally so boring and predictable and this was so out of the blue." She turned around and looked at me intently with her large pale blue eyes, as if noticing me for the first time.

"I need a bit more excitement than I think he can give me, but he is a very nice man and he's good to me, so I don't know what to do…" She looked pleadingly at me, as if I might have the answer.

"You know," I said, "most girls would love to have a fellow get down on one knee and propose with a diamond ring. They would think it was very exciting."

"I suppose so." She looked unconvinced. "I love him but I'm so bored with our relationship. He's a scientist and all he can think about is test tubes and formulas. There's only one place where we really connect and even that has been boring lately. I need something … more." She was barely concealing her frustration. I'm used to people divulging intimate details within moments of meeting me. I must have one of those non-judgemental auras. I think being "mature" and "experienced" also helps. There was no way she would have been talking to a twenty-five-year-old like this.

"I really don't want to lose him," she said, sighing, "so I better go home and make up with him. Find me something sexy that will help make everything all right."

She looked around the shop and appeared to really see what was in the store for the first time. I noticed that her eyes lingered on a display of silk slips and cami/knicker sets. She had an easy figure to fit; slender-waisted with full hips, slim legs and a medium size bust. She settled on a black silk teddy with red lace inserts and shoestring straps. Very sophisticated and sexy.

As I wrapped it in tissue, I wished her good luck and hoped that things turned out well.

Two weeks later she was back. The teddy had done the trick, she said, and things had been okay for the first couple of days … but then he went back to being boring. However, they had had an argument this morning and she needed more lingerie—maybe something in pink this time. I asked her if she had accepted the proposal, and if I could see the ring. Women find a very appreciative audience in me. I love looking at jewellery, and there is something special about the look in a woman's eye as she shows off her engagement ring.

She shook her head as she showed me a bare ring-finger. "No. We still have a lot to sort out. That's why we're arguing." She chose a transparent silk chiffon chemise in pale pink with frills over the bust that ruffled with every movement she made and a matching G-string.

This pattern repeated three times over the next couple of months. They would argue and she would come in and buy something sexy to help with the "making up" process. However, her finger remained bare, and it didn't seem as if she were moving towards a decision about whether or not to accept his proposal. He was still as boring and predictable as ever, but she was enjoying the arguments. Making up was far more exciting than the rest of the relationship.

Over a month later she came in again. I commented on the fact that I hadn't seen her for a while and asked if things had settled down.

"Well," she said, looking mischievous. "It's like this. You're right. We haven't had an argument since the last time I was here, and I'm bored to tears. He thinks it's wonderful that we're getting on so well and wants to set a date to get married. So we made plans for dinner tonight at a nice restaurant so we can discuss it." Her eyes sparkled in anticipation. She obviously had something exciting to share.

"That's when we're going to have an argument. I've got it all planned. We won't even get to eat dessert. All I need is the lingerie—I'll be dessert. I think something in red will make this argument very special."

She went straight to the rack containing the red bras and chose a red lace quarter cup bra. She liked the idea of having the bra just cup her breasts from underneath, with her nipples exposed—it's the bra you wear when you want to look like you aren't wearing a bra.

She added the matching G-string and suspender belt to the pile of things that were going to make her Machiavellian scheme work. The stockings were a very sheer eight-denier black with a red Cuban heel and seam and a red satin band at the top. She was planning to wear them with a black-and-red wrap dress held together with a tie at the side and black pumps with six-inch heels. She had everything planned.

She knew at what point during dinner to start the argument and what they were going to argue about, whether he liked it or not. She knew when she was going to demand that they leave and where exactly during the taxi ride home she was going to "accidentally" cross her legs so that her dress would ride up and he would see the top of her stockings. Then she would lean forward to show off the top of her breasts, exposed in the quarter cup. She was becoming quite flushed just talking about it.

"You realise you can't base a marriage on make-up sex," I said. After she had shared so much of her personal life with me, I was really hoping that her relationship would work out—but she was making dangerous choices if she wanted the relationship to survive.

"Who wants to get married? I'm well over that idea. Right now, all I'm doing is living from argument to argument. All the rest of it is just existing. This is the most fun I've had since we met."

She was almost quivering with excitement at the thought of the night ahead.

"How does he feel about it?" I asked, knowing that this could not continue for much longer.

She was wearing lingerie like a suicide bomber—prepared to blow up the relationship for no other reason than the impossible idea of constant perfect, angry sex. Lingerie is usually used by women to help maintain a good relationship or to spice one up. Sometimes it's used to repel advances. In this case, she was using lingerie as a weapon. She had the power; and silks and satins were her weapons. She saw no future and had no thought for the consequences beyond her immediate gratification. And the poor fellow obviously had no idea what was happening. There was no way that this was going to last.

"He hasn't quite figured out what's going on. But it's not as if he isn't getting something out of it." She shrugged, as though trying to justify actions that she knew were cruel, deliberate and impossible to sustain. Nothing was going to change her mind; she was incapable of seeing beyond her own needs for erotic pleasure. She paid for her items and left, twirling her bag of love-killing lingerie round her fingers like a baton.

About a year later, she came into the shop again, and I noticed that her finger was still bare.

"What happened?" I asked.

"Oh… It was a complete disaster," she said sadly. "I was so humiliated. He'd figured out what I was doing and had enough and moved out that night. I thought I was in control of the whole relationship. I was so wrong. I just got so caught up in it all." she shook her head as she spoke.

"I hear he met someone else and they are already engaged. The thing is, I never realised how much I really loved him till I heard he found someone else," she said regretfully. "I just thought he would come back to me."

"Oh well. I guess all I need now is a beige T-shirt bra…"

Chapter 7

Who knows where or when

She was so hunched up it seemed like her shoulders were whispering secrets into her ears. And the secrets made her sad. The weight of the world was on her shoulders, and the only way she could deal with it was by pushing them higher, as if fighting back.

After losing some weight and going through menopause, she needed a new bra. About my height, she was pretty with short blonde hair, fair skin, expressive blue eyes and full lips that looked like they hadn't smiled in a long time. Although not slender, she looked fit and toned. I took a quick visual measurement and led her to the rack with her size.

"How about this pretty cream lace one?"

The bra featured ivory lace over peach-coloured satin, with soft straps about 1.5 cm wide. I chose a balconette style because the side support on the bra was very firm, that meant that the shoulder straps could be left loose. There would be no added pressure on her shoulders.

She glanced over at the door and said "just one moment" as she stepped outside to have a chat with a tall, elegant, elderly gentleman who seemed to be waiting for her. He placed a concerned hand on her shoulder as they talked. The connection between them was obvious; he didn't seem to want to leave, but finally nodded and left.

When she came back in, I led her to the change room and waited till she was ready for me to check the size. The bra fit perfectly over the bust, but I wanted to let out the straps on the shoulder to make it more comfortable. As I was doing so, I noticed that one shoulder was much higher than the other. I showed her by putting a finger on each shoulder; when she checked in the mirror, she could see the difference.

"I carry all my stress in my shoulders," she said sadly. "I get weekly massages to try to loosen the muscles, but it doesn't really help."

"Why are you stressed?" I asked.

Most people love the opportunity to unload their problems on a stranger, and when they are undressed and more vulnerable than usual, a sympathetic enquiry can help them to unleash all their pain and sorrow. And I'm a good listener.

"There has been no light in my life ever since my beloved Donald died."

Her head and neck seemed to sink further into her shoulders. Her eyes half-closed in sadness and she took a deep breath, as if saying the words made it real—and for her, reality was not a wonderful place. She had been married to the love of her life for twenty-six wonderful years, she told me, but he had died suddenly and now she was alone. Each day was agony and filled with sorrow. She was missing half of herself. However, life had to go on, as did the business they had built together. There was no choice. The sun rose each day and there was no escape from either her sadness or her responsibilities.

I am often confronted with people's pain. My customers seem to sense my empathy and tell me the most intimate details of their lives at every opportunity. The trust that they place in me, not only to find the perfect fit but also to not judge their lives, is a great honour. I have experienced both triumph and tragedy in my life, but have always tried to maintain a positive outlook and find the humour in everything. It's not always easy!

People deal with tragedy in different ways. Some put everything behind them quickly, and others go through a process of mourning before finding a reason to smile again. As there was obviously no smile to be found here, I instead set about finding her the prettiest bra in the shop. Women are strange creatures. We can be sad and depressed, but putting on something pretty and a bit of lippy can give us a lift and help us face the day.

She chose two bras in the end. As she paid, I remembered something that a dear friend of mine had told me after my first marriage ended and my father died in the same week.

"Grief will become like the lines in your hand," I told her. "They are a part of you—etched into your very being. Every now and then you will look at them, but most days you just get on with it and not even notice they are there."

She took hold of my hand and turned it over to check out my lines.

"See?" I said. "They are still there, but life has gone on."

She smiled a sad smile, said thank you and left.

Over the next few months, I saw her often around the neighbourhood, having coffee or breakfast. She was always accompanied by the elderly gentleman who had come with her to the shop that first time. They seemed to be very close, and the connection between them was strong, despite the age difference. His affection for her was neither fatherly nor romantic. It was almost as if he were her guardian angel.

The first time I bumped into them I was greeted with a smile and an invitation to join them for coffee. He was a perfect gentleman and stood to greet me when I approached their table. She introduced herself as Lorraine and the gentleman as Gabriel. He bowed slightly as his name was mentioned. However, I am always in a rush to get back to the shop, so as much as I might have liked to sit and chat, it was not possible.

They turned up at the shop again after a couple of months, and Gabriel waited respectfully outside. I invited him in and led him to one of the red leather chairs behind my desk. This time Lorraine was looking for some camisoles, so I found a couple of different styles for her to try while Gabriel and I chatted. He had a heavy European accent, so I asked where he was from. The European community that had come to Australia after the Second World War was close-knit, and I wondered if he knew any of my family.

It turned out Gabriel was Czech-born and came from a noble family that had owned a renowned horse stud in Czechoslovakia until the war began. His father went off to England to join the RAF, which made his family a Nazi target. They were hidden by friends, but after the war, when the Communists took over, they weren't treated much better than when the Nazis had been in power. In 1948, his family managed to escape and fled to Australia as refugees.

Gabriel had known Lorraine and her husband for many years; they were all partners in a food importing business. As we spoke, he constantly looked over at the change room where Lorraine was, seeming very attuned to her every movement and need. I excused myself and popped over to check how the camisoles fit. The straps needed adjusting—those tight shoulders pulled everything up high.

Lorraine asked if the first bra she had purchased from me came in any other colour, as it was very comfortable and she enjoyed wearing it. Luckily, I had it in black lace over gold satin. Even though it was the same style and size, I insisted that she try it on.

The same bra in a different colour can fit completely differently due to the dyeing process affecting the way elastics behave. And in the manufacturing process, different machinists sew with different seams and sometimes things just don't measure up the same. I am very particular about the way things fit, but in this case there was no issue and the black bra fit as well as the ivory. Lorraine decided on the black camisole to go with her new bra. The camisole was reversible—quite a clever design. The cami sat well whether worn with the V, or with the slight curve, to the front. As they left, Gabriel kissed my hand and promised to come back soon. Such old world charm!

The pair would come in every three months or so, and I noticed a slow change in Lorraine's manner. She was slowly recovering from the loss of her "greatest love". She smiled more easily and stood a little straighter. There was also a change in Gabriel's greeting. We went from the very gentlemanly kiss on the hand to something quite different! He would walk in, stand in the middle of the shop and roar with his arms outstretched until I ran into them and was enveloped by a huge bear-hug. He was very strong and it almost took my breath away, but it felt wonderful! Such a warm, affectionate hug has a way of making the world better. Sometimes, if he was in the vicinity, he would just come in for a hug and then be on his way. I loved it!

Lorraine had started swimming every day and the exercise proved cathartic. Sydney is magnificent and its beaches are spectacular, so starting every day with a swim was good for the soul. It turned out that Gabriel had moved in with her soon after her husband died so that she would not be rambling around alone in her big house. He was a wonderful companion—charming, witty, intelligent and a perfect gentleman with a cheeky sense of humour. They spent almost every minute of every day together, and life seemed to be suiting them well.

The next time they came to the shop, Lorraine wanted a new nightie. I chose a pretty rose-pink silk chemise with a matching floral robe. She tried it on, but this time she came out and modelled it for Gabriel, who clapped his hands appreciatively and asked if there were any matching frilly bits!

My relationships with my customers often evolve into real friendships. We share our lives and stories, and it's difficult in such an intimate situation to not develop genuine affection for people. I wasn't surprised to find this happening with Lorraine and Gabriel, and I always looked forward to seeing them.

One afternoon, Lorraine came in and asked if I wanted to meet for coffee after work. We set a date and I met her and Gabriel at one of the cafes near the shop. After we ordered, it became apparent they had something they wanted to share with me. She started to talk about her darling Donald, but this time the conversation soon took on a very different tone.

"You know," she said, "we were married many times, over many lives."

I listened as Gabriel told me how the three of them—Gabriel, Donald and Lorraine—were connected through many lives, across thousands of years. The trio had experienced great adventures through time, and Gabriel related how Donald had been his second-in-charge when he was an officer to the ancient Roman Emperor, Marcus Aurelius. (They had even worked together to establish the points of defence against the Gauls.) And hundreds of years later, Gabriel and Lorraine had been married in 14th-century Hungary and lived on a grand estate, but she had died young; there remained in her a great feeling of sadness.

I had never thought too deeply about reincarnation, although it is part of Jewish belief that our souls revolve through a succession of lives until we have completed all of the 613 commandments or good deeds that the Torah commands. However, I have always understood that some people have a deep, inexplicable understanding of certain things and connection to certain people that makes no real logical sense but exists nonetheless. Sometimes a new mum comes into the shop for a maternity bra with her baby, and I can tell straight away that this baby is an old soul. The mother usually smiles at me and says that, yes, this is not the first time she's heard that.

Gabriel and Lorraine had recently taken a trip to Hungary. The two of them visited a place where they felt they had been before, together, with Donald. The sensation had been very strong.

"It was incredible," Gabriel told me, "because we knew we had been there. We both felt it, and for three days after we left, we still had the feeling that we were there."

"In that life, I know I died early," Lorraine went on to explain, all the time looking at Gabriel. "I always have this vision of Gabriel walking on the estate in Hungary, in another life; you know he loves walking—that has been the same in all of his lives and is no different in this one. The people on the estate would never speak to him because they knew that he had suffered a loss and weren't quite sure how to approach him, but he walked among them anyway.

"He always wanted to know that the people on the estate were cared for and that everything was in good order. In that life, we held formal balls and informal soirees and all the gentry would come from far and wide. We also held fair days for the locals. We both have the same memories of that time. I have also had a life as a Carmelite nun in Spain, and in that life, I looked after a very close friend of Gabriel's. My lives have all been very closed and protected. There has always been someone to look after me. In fact, before Donald died, he asked Gabriel to take care of me, and he asked me to take care of Gabriel!"

"And that is what we are doing," Gabriel piped in. "We are connected on every level and we are as one in everything."

Listening to Gabriel and Lorraine, two well-spoken, intelligent and down-to-earth people, discuss their relationships in previous lives, I had no reason to doubt them. It was as if there were an invisible link that had drawn them together over different lifetimes, and so, today, they were here and closer than ever.

After many years of hard work, their business has become quite able to survive without them, so Lorraine and Gabriel decided to spend two months of every year travelling— operas in Vienna, cruises on the Nile. Lorraine hadn't had a holiday in ten years, but now they were able to enjoy every moment together. Each trip required new lingerie, of course. As time passed, the styles she needed changed. Long straps were no longer required— her shoulders finally settled into a straight, stress-free line. People they met on their travels would often question their relationship and would raise their eyebrows at the age difference. Gabriel and Lorraine would just exchange knowing smiles. Their relationship transcended space and time.

Postscript

We lost Gabriel last year at the age of ninety-two. His passing was quick and painless. I miss his hugs. Lorraine, although sad, was quite sanguine about the loss. She knows she will see him again. She just doesn't know where or when.

Chapter 8

Mummy! Mummy!

"Mummy! Mummy! Please, can we look in this shop? Please? Please!"

The voice had only just broken and was struggling to find a pitch.

"Please, can we go in?"

He rushed in before his mother had an opportunity to say no. All arms and legs, the boy was around fourteen years old, with blond hair grown long over his ears. He wore black jeans tight over his slender hips and a black T-shirt that clung to his straight, narrow shoulders. His mother followed him in, wearing a well-rehearsed, patient smile. She was quite tall, with shoulder-length blonde hair, kind eyes and an athletic body that had obviously seen many hours at the gym.

The boy went to the bras and started rummaging through them—picking up different styles and commenting on the different colours and fabrics. He finally chose one and begged his mum to try it on for him.

"Just a minute, David—first let's see if that's my size, and let me ask if it's all right." She turned to look at me. "Do you mind?"

"Of course not," I answered, and led her to the change room. David followed and hovered as she got undressed, all the time chattering away about how pretty the bra was. I didn't want to intrude; it seemed like such an intimate moment between— well, if it were between a mother and daughter it wouldn't have been like this at all. Most daughters at this age would either be embarrassed in front of their mum, looking for guidance or, in the worst case, pouty and not wanting to be involved at all. A teenage boy would NEVER come into my shop unless he HAD to before being able to go somewhere else he'd chosen—and even then, he'd likely much prefer to wait outside, playing a game on his phone. For most teenage boys, anything would be better than hanging out in a ladies' underwear shop. But not this boy.

David returned to the racks to look for more styles.

"Would you like me to check the size for you?" I asked. It seemed the right moment to enter into the conversation.

"Yes—if you wouldn't mind."

I went to the change room and saw that the size wasn't quite right. "I think you need a bigger cup size," I said, "but let's go down a size in the back at the same time. Let's look at the 10DD instead of the 12C."

"Hang on—wait for me." David came running back to the change room and ran a critical eye over his mum's bust, trying to understand why I had come to that conclusion.

"The back is a little bit loose and rides up when you tighten the shoulder strap," I explained, more to him than his mum, who seemed to have chosen the path of least resistance. "There should be a straight line from under the bust all the way round the back. At the same time, if you look at the sides, you can see your mum is coming out there and there," I pointed to the sides where her breasts were oozing out. "A smaller back size and a bigger cup size should fix all that. But if it isn't right, then we will look for a different style."

David nodded his understanding and we went to find the right size. While I was at it, I picked up another style that ought to suit if this one didn't. I handed the new size to her with a smile and she put it on. David wanted to adjust the straps for her, though, all the time commenting of the difference in the fit. She wasn't in the least bit modest in front of her son, and he seemed quite comfortable with the sight of his mum's breasts; it was more like a close mother/daughter relationship. I also handed her the second style as well so we could get a comparison. This one was a better fit.

"I prefer the way that this one sits," I told them. "Each breast is slightly different on everyone, and a plunge bra can sometimes exaggerate that difference. But this bra, which is more of a balconette style, sits a lot better."

"Oh—I can see that now," David said. "Mummy, do you like it? I'm going to see what there is to match."

He chose the G-string over the panties and handed them to her. I changed the size and explained that even though she was a size 12, the fabric used in this style has very little stretch, so a size 14 would be more comfortable. He was fascinated by the concept of stretch in the different fabrics, and so I showed him what I meant by taking both sizes and opening them up as much as possible and then taking a different style with a fabric that had more elastic and comparing them. He was soaking up all this information like a sponge. His mother was very quiet through the whole exchange, quite happy to let him ask as many questions as he needed, obviously not interested in stifling his curiosity. She purchased the set and they left.

I ran into them a number of times over the next few months while having coffee at my local café. She told me her name was

Karen. She was married and had two other sons—both older—but I never saw any of them out with her, just David.

About six months later, they came in again. David seemed different. There was a brittle edge that had entered his voice. He seemed to be trying to control his voice more and raise its pitch, but his body was betraying him. They looked through the pyjamas this time, but there wasn't anything they wanted and so they left.

I ran into them quite a few times over the following year— often in the middle of the week, during school hours, which I thought was quite odd. His father and brothers were nowhere to be seen, and he seemed to be hanging off his mother's arm with a greater sense of desperation. A lot of the chattiness had disappeared as well, and Karen's eyes seemed to be quite sad.

The next time they came in, David's hair was quite long and pulled back in a ponytail. He seemed to be growing into his body a lot better—taller and broader shoulders but still very slender and wearing the same style of skinny black jeans and a tight T-shirt. He was also sporting a very light growth of dark hair on his upper lip. He went to look at the bras, but instead of looking for Karen's size, he was searching for the A cups. He found one he liked and asked if he could try it on. I looked at Karen, and she gave a tiny imperceptible nod. Her eyes pleaded with me to say yes.

I went with him to the change room and asked if he would mind if I helped him to put the bra on. He was quite comfortable with his mum's body, but I wasn't sure he was with his own. He had chosen the worst style for his shape—he was, of course, flat-chested, and even though the bra was an A cup, it stood away from his chest wall and there was air in between. I have a lot of customers who are very small in the bust or who have had mastectomies, and there are certain styles that suit them more than others—but the same goes for any size. If it were simple, I would only have one style in the shop and that would be it. As it is, I have dozens of styles and over sixty bra sizes. The art is in being a matchmaker—the perfect bra with the perfect fit.

I also noticed something quite disturbing. David had a big blue bruise on his back and a smaller one on his side, as well as lots of small, healed cuts across his belly and some recent ones that were an angry red and scabbed. I looked at Karen and raised my eyebrows.

"His brothers have been picking on him and he's been badly bullied at school," she said quietly.

That explained why I had seen him out and about on so many school days. They were looking for a way to home-school him. He was obviously very bright, but the school environment was dangerous for him. This was a tragedy waiting to happen. I asked about her husband and how he was dealing with it.

"As far as he's concerned," Karen said, "he has three sons. Not two sons and a daughter but three sons. That's it. No discussion. He just doesn't want to talk about it. End of conversation. I wasn't prepared to accept his view or let him force David to be something he wasn't, so we've split up now." She looked so heartbroken at having broken up her family, but she was determined to stand by and protect David no matter what. "We were hoping to have a gender reassignment operation soon but his shrink won't let him do anything till he's at least eighteen."

"That's two more years, Mum—how will I cope?" David moaned, near tears.

"Listen, darling," I said. Calling him David seemed so inappropriate now. "Listen to your shrink. I know it's hard, but they know what they're doing. In the meantime, there is one very important thing you need to do right now if you want to be a beautiful woman. Stop cutting yourself immediately. Those cuts will leave scars, and one day you'll want to wear a midriff top or even a bikini and those scars will get in the way. They'll just be an awful reminder of a time when you were unhappy. In the meantime, buy some vitamin E oil and rub it in every day. It will help them fade." I could see the gratitude in Karen's eyes. I could only imagine how difficult this must all be for her.

We found a pretty lace crop-top with triangle cups with a little bit of padding in pink. David wanted the white one as well, but Karen said they couldn't afford it—there was still so much to work out with the divorce.

I didn't see them for about a year after that. They must have moved from the neighbourhood. Then, one day, he came in by himself—but there was a big change. He sashayed in wearing a short, tartan, pleated skirt that swung around his hips as he walked and black ankle boots with a small heel. His hair had been cut into a shoulder-length bob, and he was constantly fiddling with it—pushing it behind his ear as it fell into his eyes. I noticed he was wearing eyeliner and lip gloss as well. He was still wearing a tight T-shirt but now there were two definite breasts showing—small, sure, but they were there. He noticed me looking, threw his shoulders back and grinned.

"Guess what! I'm taking hormones now and I'm having my op in six months when I turn eighteen." His voice was higher—not quite feminine yet, but the intonation of the words definitely was. The features on his face also seemed to be softer and fuller. The hair growth on his upper lip had also disappeared. I told him all that I noticed and was rewarded with a huge smile.

"Oh, and by the way, allow me to introduce myself. My name is Dahlia," she said with a small curtsy.

"Such a pretty name! It really suits you."

What an amazing transformation! The haunted look had disappeared. In its place was joy, a proud sense of self and optimism. We looked for a new bra together—I found some B cups that were suitable for small, wide busts. Dahlia wanted something in red, but I thought that the shade of red I had in stock then—a Lipstick Red as opposed to a Tango Red—was too pink for her skin and wouldn't look nice, so we looked for shades of blue instead. We gossiped liked a couple of old girlfriends; I commented on how well the scars were fading. Apparently, Bio-oil worked better than the straight Vitamin E and smelt nicer as well. I admired the way she applied her eyeliner; I can never get my line to be quite that straight.

"Practice makes perfect," she giggled.

I shared with her my grandmother's secret for how to not get lipstick on your teeth: when you've finished applying it you pucker your lips around your finger like a kiss and then slowly pull your finger out. Any extra lipstick ends up on your finger and not your teeth. I made a silly faux-sexy face as I showed her how to do it. Dahlia thought my grandmother was a genius. I also told her that she insisted that I not let a boy kiss me because I might get pregnant. We laughed at how Grandma was worried about me getting pregnant but showed me how to do naughty things with my finger.

After trying on a few different styles, we selected the perfect one. It was a French import, so it cost a lot more than the usual. When it came time to pay, Dahlia called her father so he could transfer some money into her account. She flirted with him over the phone and gave him a big kiss down the line when he finally agreed to the price.

I guess he finally got used to having a daughter—and a whole new conversation was just beginning.

Chapter 9

Clumsy

"Clumsy!" I thought to myself as the woman walked through the shop. With a large and obviously heavy backpack on her back, she managed to send bras and knickers flying each time she circled the racks of my well-stocked shop.

I walked behind her, picking up items as they fell. "Would you like to pop your backpack down in the corner there?" I asked. "It might make it easier to see things." I smiled at her so as not to make her feel embarrassed for her lack of gracefulness.

She nodded and placed her backpack in the corner—almost tripping over her own feet as she went. The backpack was straining at the zips from being overpacked; there was a small pink teddy bear tied to the strap, a note attached to its head saying "WE LOVE YOU MUMMY" in a childish scrawl. She looked very ill—and ill at ease. Puffy and pale, she was in her late twenties and was wearing an oversized black T-shirt and trackpants. Her face was somewhat featureless—full cheeks, small lips that didn't seem to smile easily and stringy, mousey blonde hair tied back in a ponytail. She wore absolutely no make-up—not even lip gloss—and appeared not to care about her appearance at all.

"Can I help you with your size?" I asked her.

"I'm not sure what I am. I've just put on a bit of weight, so it's all changed," she replied, her voice soft and shaky.

"What are you looking for?" I took a quick measurement and told her she was about a 12D for the bra and between a 14 and 16 around the hips, depending on the style. Sizes, of course, vary between the styles and the brands, but it was a good place to start.

She went straight to the rack with all the red bras on it and picked up the sexiest see-through bra and handed it to me. "Something like this," she said. Then she rifled through the rack some more and pulled out a garter belt that resembled a micro mini skirt, one that would barely cover anything. "I also want something like this, but without the stocking attachments."

Not what I was expecting her to say, but I went about finding her size. I showed her how the suspender attachments on the skirtini could be removed. The skirting had three rows of ruffles at the back and a single frill layer that went all the way around. She shook it on the hanger to see how it moved and then, pleased with the choice, went to the change room to try them on—but not before pulling out her phone from her backpack, checking for messages and asking if it would be safe where she left it.

I assured her that it would be fine there and closed the curtain so she could change in privacy. After a couple of minutes, I asked if she was happy with the size. She wasn't sure, so I opened the curtain to see how she was going. She had the bra on, and after checking that the bra fit from all angles, I adjusted the strap to give her a bit more lift. She also needed to adjust her nipple position in the bras, as one had drifted off to the left. I showed her how to drop into a bra. You need to bend forward and shake your shoulders until your boobs move. That way they drop in front of the wire and everything fits better. When you're young, you're taught to lift your boobs up into the bra cup with your hands. That works well when you're firm, but as you get older and your shape changes and lowers, if you use that method you can empty out close to the wire and the top of the breast may spill out.

She seemed happy with the fit and commented on how firm her boobs looked in the bra considering she had breastfed two babies. However, her face seemed to show no joy as she mentioned the children. Her shoulders visibly slumped, and she sighed and said she would try on the skirtini.

I left her to disrobe, but I could hear her struggling to take off her trackpants and pull the skirtini on. I had left her two sizes— the 14 and the 16—and told her that she should probably go for the larger size so it wouldn't pull tight across her hips. If it was too tight, I explained, it would then ride up and sit on the waist, and it would look better if it sat on her hips. She knocked the mirror twice and apologised for it. I laughed and said that everybody does it and she shouldn't worry about it.

"My husband put up those mirrors when I opened the shop," I explained. "He has a very expensive, fully-equipped toolbox, which he proudly wheeled into the shop. He spent over an hour measuring and drilling and nailing the mirrors into place. I told him they were crooked. He looked at them and then decided that it didn't matter, anyway, as he would happily volunteer to be the mirror. Needless to say, the mirrors are still crooked!"

After a few minutes, she stepped out of the change room and stood in front of the large antique mirror in the middle of the shop so she could get a better view of herself. She was a typical pear shape—narrow shoulders and waist with ample hips and big thighs. Very curvy and feminine. She was wearing the skirtini, which barely covered her rather round bottom, and her legs were bare. I realised why she didn't want the attachment for stockings. Her legs were covered with tattoos.

From the tip of her toes to the top of her rather heavy thighs were tropical flowers—hibiscus and orchids in bright reds and pinks surrounded by intertwined green leaves. The flowers were adorned with diamante piercings that made the colours sparkle. I even noticed a small, colourful bird about to take flight on the back of her left knee. It had a green crystal stud for an eye. Each toenail was painted in either red or pink to match the colours in the tattoo. The red in the bra and skirtini set off the red hibiscus flowers, and she seemed quite pleased with her reflection in the mirror. The skin on her midriff and arms was very pale, and the contrast with the lingerie and tattoos on her legs was quite striking.

She started to twirl and bend over in an attempt to look sexy. However, her body was not lithe, and her movements were jerky and clumsy—more like a child trying to copy something she had seen than a grown woman who understood the sensual possibilities of her body. No matter how hard she tried or what position she put herself in, she didn't look provocative in any way—more like a sad circus act. However, she seemed to be quite pleased with her reflection in the mirror and asked if I had the same outfit but in a hot pink to match the other flowers, or even a green to match the leaves. I had something similar in a pink and black lace, so she went to try it on.

She came out again to check how she looked in the mirror and noticed that when she bent over, she would need some underwear that covered her buttocks, as they remained untattooed and looked very pale and dimpled. I found her a sheer black bikini that fit her well, and she went back to posing in front of the mirror.

I felt uncomfortable watching her; it was quite a sad little display, as if she were desperately trying to be something she wasn't. Soon she seemed to tire from the effort of all the twisting and turning. With one last attempt to arch her back, she bent over to try and touch her toes (she could only reach her mid-calf, and she almost lost her balance as she extended forward), she stood up straight and plodded back to the change room, just as her mobile phone started ringing. She picked it up and I could hear her talking to her mum. She sounded angry and frustrated and was trying not to yell as she demanded to speak to her daughter.

"Yes, darling, I love you too," I heard her say in a softer, sweeter voice. "I promise I'll be home at the end of the week. You be a good girl for Grandma and look after your brother. Give him a big kiss from me and remember I love you all to bits." She was obviously upset by talking to her children, and I could hear her voice catch in her throat—but it then became stronger as she continued the conversation with her mother. "Don't tell me what I can and can't do—I have to do this, Mum. We've already been through this a hundred times. I thought you understood. It's too late now. It's done." She was almost yelling by this point, and I heard her slam the phone down on the chair in the change room.

After a few minutes she came out, looking more composed. She placed the two sets on the table and asked how much they would be. I gave her the total, which came to nearly $400. She looked stricken at the amount but went to her backpack and pulled out her wallet, first giving the little teddy bear with the note a glance and then a gentle caress. She carefully counted out the cash from her wallet, placing all the notes and coins on the table before realising she didn't have enough. She pulled out a credit card and gingerly handed it over, stating that she hoped it had enough credit on it.

"I've come down from the country to Sydney." She slumped over the desk, exhausted from the effort of trying on the lingerie and distraught over the phone conversation. In a quiet but determined voice, she continued, "Somebody told me that with these tattoos on my legs, I shouldn't have any problems getting a job as a dancer".

Her story was important, and she needed to tell it on her terms. She looked me directly in the eyes and went on, her voice gaining strength and a sense of purpose.

"You see, I've just been given a terminal diagnosis. I've got leukaemia and the chemo hasn't worked, so the doctors think I've got about six months left. I reckon if I get a job stripping for a week or two, I should be able to get enough money together to take the kids to Disneyland. One last happy memory before I get too sick to do anything with them."

The credit card was approved, and I wrapped her purchases in red tissue paper. I watched her stuff the parcel in the backpack, and as she was leaving, I said, "If you change your mind ... just bring it all back with the tags on, and I'll give you a full refund."

She looked at me and smiled a sad little smile as she straightened her shoulders to take the weight of the backpack. She turned around and walked out the door.

Chapter 10

Apparently, I'm fat

I never wanted to have a baby. Don't get me wrong; I think that being a parent is one of the most wonderful things that anyone can do. I watch all my friends with their children and the way their expressions change when they talk about them. Such feelings of happiness and pride! There is a special word for it in Yiddish: *nachas* (pronounced with a guttural *ch*, like you've got something stuck in your throat, like tears of joy). I love listening to their stories about their progeny—the good marks at school, the funny things they say, how well they play the piano, the times they fall over and break a bone but never fall on their face. G-d forbid, after all the money spent on their teeth! They start "*shpritsing with nachas*" (spraying their *nachas* so much I feel like I need a raincoat or at least an umbrella!) How they love being with their children and resent the fact that one day, all too soon, their kids will prefer to be with their friends and then eventually go to university, maybe in another town, or get married and move far away and they'll never see them and … and … and…

I've never wanted that joy OR that worry. I don't think I'm cut out for it, and it's way too important a thing to do to if you're not 100% committed. It's going to change your life in every way.

Nothing will ever be the same. Your life, your body, your relationship with your partner, your family, your friends, your finances—it all changes, and in ways that nothing and no-one could ever prepare you for. Everyone tells me that once you hold your baby in your arms, you will love them. Then they tell me for sure that I would make a fantastic mum. But there are no guarantees. I've met enough women who have confided in me that that is not necessarily the case. It's not that they don't love their kids; it's just that they hate "motherhood" and everything it entails. They feel they've been conned because the promised maternal feelings never eventuated. And then there are those who feel that being a mum defines them and has empowered them to be and do things they never thought possible. It's like their superpower.

I have managed to pour whatever maternal feelings I have into my dogs. I remember walking down a street with a girlfriend who was pining for another baby. We saw a mother carrying her newborn and my friend almost melted. She yearned for another one of her own. Further up the street we saw a puppy and I started to spontaneously projectile lactate! There it is. To each her own...

"Apparently I'm fat."

Sophia's eyes welled up with tears and her body shook from emotion.

I put my arm around her and pulled her in close for a big hug. She wasn't what I would call "fat", not by any stretch of the imagination—maybe a little curvy and round, but the figure was definitely hourglass, with a slim waist and full hips and an ample bust. Her body went in, stayed there for a bit and then back out, just like a woman is meant to. I thought she looked quite lovely and lush.

After a few moments, the tears subsided. Taking her hand, I led her to the chairs behind my desk. I handed her the box of tissues and got her a glass of water.

"Who said you're fat?" I asked after she had calmed down.

"My husband. I don't understand why he would say that. I had my baby six months ago and I'm already back to my pre-pregnancy weight."

"Are you breastfeeding?" I asked.

"No—it didn't work out. My boobs grew huge when I was pregnant, and they haven't gone back to how they were before. Maybe that's what he hates. I don't understand." The weeping started again. Sophia's body had always performed well for her. A faithful servant. It had brought her pleasure and plenty. Falling pregnant had been effortless and the pregnancy itself was uneventful, as was childbirth. But here she was with the longed-for baby, and the much-anticipated breastfeeding had been difficult. All she was left with were the boobs to remind her of her failure.

Even through the tears, Sophia was pretty. Large brown eyes rimmed by long lashes, pale clear skin and shoulder-length straight black hair. She was in her early thirties and was dressed in loose-fitting black pants and a frumpy, oversized top. The baggy clothes did little to enhance her figure. There had been no care taken in her choice of clothes that day. She wore no make-up. It was as if she took no pride in her appearance at all; whatever self-esteem she had left had been destroyed by her husband's cruel words. She appeared to be both emotionally and physically exhausted and filled with unaccustomed self-loathing.

"So, how can I help you?" I asked.

"Maybe it's all this he hates," she said, pulling at her oversized clothes, which she seemed to be wearing as a shield against her husband's disdain. How could he not love the body that had given birth to his child? "I'm still wearing my maternity bra and it's horrible. It gives me no shape and it's so damn ugly."

"They can be quite awful," I said. "And when they stretch out and go saggy-baggy, they look like men's Y-fronts, and we all know how ugly they are." At least that got her to smile. "All right—let's get you into something better and we'll see how you feel then."

I took a quick measurement of her bra size and led her to the change room before going to find her a pretty, purple bra with a matching boy short to try on. She had always been a C-cup, but the pregnancy had changed her size and now she was wearing a very full DD. However, her bust was very high and her shape was beautiful. She looked like one of the well-endowed actresses of the 1950s. I told her she could still pass the pencil test. She'd never heard of it.

"That's what we used to do when I was in high school in the 1970s," I explained. "You would put a pencil under your breast and if it fell out, that meant you had good breasts, but if your breasts drooped a bit, the pencil would stay in place and you failed. I was so big-busted even then that I failed the pencil-case test. I could hold a whole pencil case in place and would have to send a search party in to find it."

She laughed, and I could see that she was starting to calm down. I found her another set in black lace as well as a beautiful pyjama set in a floral chiffon that had long, loose drawstring pants and a matching cami-top which was low cut and perfectly cupped her breasts. She admired her reflection in the mirror, and the change was immediate. Her posture improved; so did her mood. For the first time in ages, she was able to see herself as a beautiful shapely woman and not a lump. A journey had been undertaken from self- loathing to the determination to be fabulous. She looked and felt wonderful, and we decided that there was no way that her husband could say she looked fat now.

As I wrapped all her purchases, we made a pact. She was going to go home and throw out all her horrible, old, ill-fitting underwear and parade around the house in her new lingerie. She threw her arms around me and gave me a big hug as she thanked me.

Three weeks later, Sophia was back.

"Apparently I'm still fat—but now he tells me I'm ugly, too." The tears did not flow this time. However, I could feel her anger.

"Hang on," I said, "there's something else going on here". Any man who can look at the mother of his firstborn child and undeservedly disparage her looks, especially when she's making a concerted effort to appear attractive to him, has something on his mind that has nothing to do with her appearance.

"Didn't he want the baby?" I asked.

"He thought he did. We've been married for six years and things were fine. I can't say that we were a perfect couple, but opposites attract. I'm organised and a bit of a workaholic and he's not. But he always made me laugh and got me to not take myself too seriously. I've seen marriages a helluva lot worse than ours," she explained with a sigh while loosening the clip that held her hair back in a stern bun. It was obviously as heavy on her head as her predicament was on her life

"We talked about it and planned for it with my work." She continued while fluffing out her hair so it fell in soft waves to her shoulder. "I organised to take maternity leave for six months, and he was to go and get a better paying job, because my big salary wasn't going to be coming in in the same way—and we all know how expensive babies are. But now he has to grow up and get a real job, and it seems that it's all too hard for him. I've always earned more money than he did, but it was never a problem. He liked the lifestyle—not having to worry about anything and spending all his time down the pub with his mates and doing odd jobs for a bit of cash."

"I didn't mind too much." She shrugged as she explained. "I loved him and didn't want to be one of those women who picked a man so they could change them. It all seemed okay, but I guess I just didn't think it through. Now that I have to stay at home to look after the baby, he has to grow up and act like a man and a father. But he doesn't want to be a stay-at-home dad, either. He just wants to do what *he* wants to do, without any responsibility." She was getting angrier as she went on. Resignation and regret were morphing into indignation and recognition of the reality of her situation.

He needs to grow up, but now I realise… It. Will. Never. Happen. EVER!" She said each word slowly for effect and finished with a roar—she knew it to be true, but it was too life-altering to accept quietly. "He obviously prefers having a beer with the boys than having a baby with me," she added. "I'm to blame for getting pregnant and ruining his lifestyle. In other words, he had to finally be a man, and it's all my fault. I think he hates me, and even worse, he hates our baby."

"So, what are you going to do?" I asked.

"Well, it's obvious he doesn't love me, and he doesn't want to be a father, so what do I need him for? You just don't know when you get married, do you." She shrugged and then pursed her lips as she continued.

"We were so young. My mum tried to warn me, and I suppose the signs were there, but I loved him. Who knew he would turn out to be such a useless dud of a man? No, not a man. A child. A fully grown, immature, dependant, six-foot-tall, lazy, good-for-nothing child. A child I don't need. I've got a son who I love and who needs me, and that's who I have to concentrate on. I've had to make some quick and difficult decisions." As she spoke, I could feel her resolve grow. She didn't have the luxury of time to contemplate how deeply devastated she was by these unforeseen circumstances. There was no possibility of falling into a heap or even feeling sorry for how her life had turned out. Like so many strong women before her, she reached down deep inside and found that great reserve of strength and resolve to do what had to be done. Mourning a bad marriage could come later. Now she had to take care of business. The resolve in her eyes was mirrored by the determination in her voice.

"I've been in touch with my old boss, and she said I can work from home till my baby is old enough for day care. So, I don't need that useless so-and-so for anything at all! If he doesn't think I'm the best thing that's ever happened to him, then he doesn't deserve me, and he definitely doesn't deserve our baby. He's going away this weekend on a fishing weekend with his buddies, so I'm going to pack his bags and change the locks. He can move in with his buddy, and that will be the best for everyone. I just don't need him in my life. But when I tell him this, I want to feel strong and at my best, so I think I need to wear something special."

Colour affects us in so many ways. When customers come in and tell me they want underwear for a first date, I always suggest soft pastel colours—nothing too overt. It should be feminine and make them feel pretty. For a third date, we go to stronger colours; for weekends away, it's definitely black, lacy and sophisticated. I can plan seductions in every colour under the sun. However, for a job interview or an argument, when you need to feel powerful and completely in control, there's only one colour to wear—and that colour is red. Strong, vibrant and in-charge RED. Ready for anything RED. Don't mess with me RED. I'm Queen of the World RED. In charge of my own destiny RED.

"What about this one?" I asked, showing Sophia a sheer red lace balcony push-up bra with vertical seams for lift and narrow, wide-set, double satin spaghetti straps. The top of the bra had a scalloped edge, embellished with silver metallic embroidery. It was a real "I'm the boss lady here and don't you forget it" bra. She admired her reflection in the mirror; her breasts sat high and firm. The matching shorts had a lace-up feature on the back waistband in the matching silver metallic ribbon contrast.

Her eyes lit up and she clapped her hands in appreciation. "I'll wear that with a pair of jeans and a white linen shirt tied at the waist so he can see the bra. Me and my baby will be so much better off without him."

I was amazed at her transformation. Her sense of self-worth seemed to return before my very eyes. She stood up straight, thrusting her shoulders back and her breasts forward. She put her hands on her hips and stood with her legs slightly apart. Strong. Resolute. Unbreakable. She was thinking clearly and was determined to do the right thing, by both her baby and herself. Like so many great women before her, adversity had only made her stronger and more determined than she ever imagined she needed to be.

Everything went to plan. Sophia threw him out. He moved in with his friend and the two of them continued the life of grown-up adolescents. She started to work from home. She hadn't realised what a drain he was on her life till he left—but without him, her life was so much smoother and easier. She managed to pay her mortgage, buy a new car and look after herself and her baby without any help from him. She knew she wasn't fat or ugly—that the problem and loss was all his.

And she figured out the ultimate revenge. She organised for him to babysit and then went over to his place and seduced his flatmate ... wearing the same red bra set she'd worn when she booted him from her life.

Chapter 11

Dance the fandango

I have a fan. It's a beauty! Shiny black ostrich feathers, each about twelve inches long, attached to a black lacquer frame. I remember the first time I saw it, in a catalogue for burlesque items, and I knew I had to have it—that somehow it would change my life. The thought of those feathers fluttering in front of my face evoked a bygone era of exotic seductions and grand loves. I imagined myself a courtesan at the opera in Paris, hoping the king would notice me as I coquettishly batted my eyelashes at him from behind my fan. Or perhaps a tango dancer in Brazil, who used it as a prop in her seductive dance. I waited in anticipation for it to be delivered. It finally arrived, beautifully packed in its own cardboard container to protect the glorious feathers when it wasn't in use. I gently took it out of the case, opened it with a flick of my wrist, and then waved it in front of my face.

I danced the Fandango.

I have lots of customers who like to come in with family and make a girly day out of buying bras. They make a day of it—

lunch at one of the local cafes and then off for a lingerie spree. It's always interesting watching the dynamic between mothers and daughters. Generally, the mothers love to see their daughters in beautiful lingerie, while the daughters have to encourage their mums to indulge themselves with something special. Maria and Debra had been coming to me for about six years. Maria came first—a vivacious blonde in her late twenties with a neat figure and 10DD bust. We had so much fun that she vowed to come back with her mum, who had always found bra buying unpleasant. She finally managed to corral Debra for a visit and we all spent a very enjoyable hour together finding the perfect style for Debra.

Debra was an attractive blonde (I could see where Maria got her looks from) in her early fifties, and her body had started to change, as it does for all peri-menopausal women. Your breasts get larger but the tissue spreads wider so seeming to start under the arm. They also drop meaning a lot of the fullness at the top of the breast migrates south to the bottom of the breast. It's just Mother Nature having a laugh. I asked Debra if she had experienced any symptoms yet of menopause, but other than her shape changing and irregular periods, she'd experienced no real symptoms. She hoped to sail through it.

"Don't we all!" I responded, with a silent prayer that I wouldn't have a problem with it myself. I hate being hot at the best of times, and the thought of hot flushes filled me with mortal fear. I asked Debra if she knew how her own mother had coped with it. Well, of course in those days nobody spoke about such things, so she had no idea—they talked about going through "the change" but wouldn't elaborate on any symptoms. Ladies of that generation thought it a virtue to suffer in silence. My own mother never talked about it and changed the subject if I asked. The more I pressed her on it, the more she seemed to become obsessed with the weather!

I smiled at Debra as I led her to the change room. "Let's go check the lay of the land, so to speak."

It turned out her new size was a 10F. I found an exotic black lace plunge bra; she was thrilled with the shape it gave her. She had recently bought a black floral wrap dress and the bra would go perfectly with the low neckline.

Maria and Debra came to the shop together about every six months after that. During that time, Debra ended up with all the symptoms of menopause. They hit her with full force. The whole catastrophe. Weight gain. Insomnia with night sweats. Anxiety. Hair loss. Itchy skin. Rage. And, of course, hot flushes. She went straight onto hormone replacement therapy—she saw no need to martyr herself to the cause. Toughing it out like some of her friends had done seemed ridiculous. The regimen worked a treat for her, and as her symptoms abated, she began to feel somewhat normal again. The medication made her breasts very full, though, and she needed resizing again. She had also completely lost her sex drive, she confided in me, but it didn't really matter anymore. Her husband had left her the year before for a younger, siliconed version. She was over the loss and quite happy with her life as it was. Family and friends, as well as her successful accountancy practice, kept her busy. The last thing she wanted at this point was a man in her life. She had no interest in "that sort of thing".

I took a quick measurement and saw that her new size was now a 12FF—a big difference from the 10F that I measured her in just a couple of years earlier. She was a little fuller across the back, and her bust had "inflated", as she described it.

"It's like I took a deep breath in and forgot to breathe out and my boobs just stayed like that," was how Debra described it to me. She was rather enjoying her matronly curves and had taken to wearing loose beaded silk caftans over jeans (with an elastic waist so she could breathe both in AND out!) rather than the more tailored dresses she had worn before. Comfort was king. She had also toned down her make-up. No more foundation and face powders for her—just a bit of mascara and tinted lip gloss was fine. She was enjoying her middle age. New hobbies were a joy. Debra had also joined a social group set up at the local yacht club and was going out and meeting new people. Life was good, and Maria was pregnant, so there was also the birth of her first grandchild to look forward to.

Debra and Maria left that day with two bras each—Debra with a simple black balconette that gave full coverage and excellent support which she liked so much she took the same style in a nude colour as well. I fitted Maria for a maternity bra and we settled on a lovely ivory lace over black satin and a red lace with black bows in a 10E. Maternity bras have come a long way since Debra was pregnant with her children, and she loved the fact that Maria could have such pretty things to wear. It's not a mutually exclusive idea to have something that is comfortable and practical, fits well and is also beautiful.

A couple of months later, I got my first peri-menopause symptom. I was hot—and not in a Marilyn Monroe kind of way, unless you're thinking about that subway grate scene in the *Seven Year Itch* where her white pleated dress is blowing up around her. I'd wake up in the middle of the night and throw off the blanket. Then I'd put it back. Then I'd throw it off again. It was winter and made no sense. I sleep with two poodles and my husband, and even though we all kind of snuggle for warmth, I'd never felt like this before. Getting back to sleep was also becoming more and more difficult. I hadn't had a period in about eighteen months, but I just thought that was natural. Then it dawned on me that maybe this could be "the change"—and if so, it wasn't that bad! I've had plenty of customers come in looking for the lightest possible cotton to sleep in because their night sweats were so bad that they had to sleep on towels, or they would soak right through to the mattress. I could live with throwing the blanket off a couple of times a night. Big deal. Piece of cake!

Oh, how foolish and naïve I was! A couple of weeks later I got my first hot flush. It started from deep inside my core and worked its way up to the top of my head. It felt like lava erupting. My skin felt damp and hot and uncomfortable, and I remember thinking, "What the hell was that?" Then it happened again a couple of hours later.

"Oh my," I thought.

And then a couple of hours again after that.

"Well, that's not fun…"

The next day I had about four again, and the day after it was six; by the next week, it was once an hour. Then I had one that seemed to go on forever. A "ROYAL FLUSH", as it were. In all the talk about Global Warming being "manmade", it seems that they forgot to recognise the real reason. It's all the fault of women having hot flushes. Typical—men taking credit for something the fairer and soggier sex has done!

By the following week, the flushes were coming at forty-five-minute intervals and I was sitting in front of my doctor in tears. I don't know how she could tell the tears from the sweat from my last flush, but she's a clever woman and must have seen this before. I didn't want to go on HRT yet, so she prescribed a herbal remedy which she said was the only one scientifically proven to work. They say that the efficacy of a medicine is in direct proportion to the confidence of the prescribing medical professional. I gave it a go on the lowest dose, and like magic, a few weeks later my flushes and middle of the night blanket chucking disappeared. I was a person again … till three months later, when

I was chatting with a customer about it; she said that when she went on the remedy, it worked for a bit and then stopped and her symptoms started up again.

Who knew I could be so suggestible? The next day, my hot flushes were back with a vengeance. I doubled the dose and it seemed to be okay for a few weeks … and then I was back to the forty-five-minute-apart hot flushes again. I intended to tough it out for as long as I could. Who cared if I never wore a scarf again? Maybe I'd just cut off my long hair and be done with it. I was sick of wearing it up. Anyway, neck scarves were so "last year"; why would anyone want to wear one? And as for hot soup … how could anyone compare a hot soup to the spine-tingling coolness of gelato! My long-suffering husband (he really is wonderful!) didn't mind that I had the air-conditioning on in the bedroom in the middle of winter. He'd come to bed in a hat and scarf and perfected the art of making himself a very small target whenever he felt the heat coming his way.

That was when I brought out my feather fan. I needed something for work that could provide me with some relief and also look fabulous. I knew that this fan would transform my life. I always kept it within arms' reach, just in case I needed to dance a Fandango. A flush would start and I'd be fanning away.

In the middle of one such flush, Debra walked in. She saw what I was doing and then her own flush started in sympathy! I came around the desk and fanned both of us at the same time. I told her that someone should plug a kettle into us and we could boil water! I got us both a couple of cold drinks from the fridge in the back and we sat together behind the counter to cool and calm down. I looked at her questioningly, as I knew she had been on HRT and wasn't having symptoms anymore.

"I have some interesting news," Debra said. "I wasn't planning on doing this, but I've met someone."

He owned a yacht—fifty feet long with a beautiful wooden interior which slept six people. He had circumnavigated Australia in it. She was fascinated by him, as he was an adventurer and marvellous raconteur, as well as a total gentleman. He had never been married, as he had always been too busy travelling the world for both business and pleasure. He even gave up smoking his much-loved cigars when she mentioned she didn't like the smell, which impressed her. He was a ridiculously handsome sixty-year-old (he resembled Sean Connery, but the bearded, more mature one, not the James Bond one), very masculine, with a high libido. That was both good and bad. Debra's hormone replacement therapy had eliminated her sex drive. Killed it dead. And here she was with Mr Gorgeous; intending to enjoy every moment with him, she had made the decision to stop taking her hormones. As expected, her libido returned, but so did her hot flushes. As a result, she needed some new lingerie that was very sexy and sophisticated but that would keep her cool.

We discussed the differences and relative qualities of padded as opposed to non-padded bras. Some of my customers who come in from Queensland and the Northern Territory like the padded bras as they soak up sweat, whereas others find that they still feel hot even if the bras are cotton-lined. We chose to go with unlined bras, and I found two beautiful sets—one bright red set from the USA which was lace and mesh over the cup, and another black set from England which had vertical seams for excellent lift and beautiful white embroidery over the top of the cups.

The other thing that Debra needed was something to sleep in. Many people believe that silk keeps them warm in winter and cool in summer. I've always found that silk makes me hot if it's woven; however, knitted silk is quite nice to wear. Of course, the most glamorous sleepwear comes in silk. Cotton is lovely to sleep in, whether it's woven or knitted; however most styles tend to be old-fashioned and in white. They look like something Granny might want to be buried in, which of course was not going to suit a seduction scene with the sexy sailor! Or there are lots of cute little pyjama sets that are perfect for teenage girls on sleepovers but NOT for a sophisticated lady spending the night with her lover.

We settled on a couple of slips made with model—one ballerina-length with high side splits, and a reversible mini-slip with a v-front and a rounded back. Model is made from beechwood and is similar to bamboo, but is a much lighter and of a finer knit. Because the fabric has about 5% elastane in the knit, it is actually quite suitable for women with bigger busts. It has a small amount of hold and stops the boobs from completely swinging in the wind, so to speak! Debra was pleased with what we had chosen and was very excited at the prospect of her "menopause affair". She had never thought to feel this way again; he had awakened feelings in her, both physical and emotional, that she had thought belonged to her past. She blushed as she spoke, but this was not a flush—it was a glow of anticipation. After two hours of trying on and four hot flushes (two for me and two for Debra), she left with two bra sets and two nightgowns . I told her that I hoped that this gentleman turned out to be everything she wanted him to be. She said she hoped so too, as Maria was thrilled about her new man and couldn't wait to meet him.

I persevered with the hot flushes for a couple more weeks, but when I took a look at my feather fan, I realised that I had to do something. It was no longer plush and beautiful. With all the fanning I was doing a lot of feathers had come loose and were crooked, and many had fallen off. It looked like a drowned chicken fan. I got my prescription for HRT and ran to the chemist to get it filled. I couldn't wait to take my first tablet, because then I would be closer to taking my second tablet and then my third and then my fourth, by which time I'd hopefully be on the way to being flush-free. It took a couple of weeks for my body to adjust to the medication, but it worked! I slept through the night without waking once, and, even better, I stopped being a walking, talking, hourly heat puddle. I was human again and oh so happy. I celebrated with a hot soup with chilli (off the menu when I was flushing) and wrapped my neck in a silk satin scarf for work the next day. I was Wonder Woman and I could handle anything! My husband lost that "scared" look and life went back to normal. I put my fan away … but not too far away, in case one of my customers walked in with a particular "glow".

About five months later, Debra dropped into the shop. I saw her and went to get my fan out of the drawer, just in case. She saw what I was doing and said, "There's no need for that anymore". I looked at her inquisitively; she shook her head sadly and said she was back on HRT again.

"We were having a great time. We went out on his yacht every weekend and saw each other a couple of times through the week. I was really falling for him. He was always so gracious and gentlemanly, and we never argued about anything. I was having the time of my life. But then he seemed to go quiet. The silences grew longer. I could tell he was trying to tell me something, but he didn't seem to have the courage. He called me up and said he wanted to see me. We sat in his lounge room making small talk for about ten minutes. I knew something was coming. Then he stood up and went over to his cabinet—opened it up and took out the biggest, fattest, stinkiest cigar. He sat next to me, knowing how much I hated them, and made a big show about lighting it. Then he blew the smoke in my face. I got furious and took the hint at the same time. Let me tell you, Pauline, I thought of you at that moment."

"Me?" I asked, quite surprised.

"Yes, you," she answered. "I wish I'd had your fan with me so I could've taken it out and fanned that disgusting smoke right back in his face. What a cowardly, disgraceful thing to do. He could've just said that it's over and that would have been okay. But to do that! No wonder he has never been married. That was just cruel." Her face screwed up in disgust as she told me this, but I could tell that she was relieved to have found this out sooner rather than later.

Debra looked around the counter and found my well-worn feather fan with its two broken feathers listing at a sad angle. She picked it up and started waving it in a slow, deliberate manner.

We danced the "FanMANgone".

Chapter 12

It ain't over till it's over

"I am not invisible. I am still a woman. I may be a 'senior' citizen—" Mum would spit out the word "senior" with such hatred and contempt, as though disbelieving how such a word could apply to her "—but I am definitely HERE and I will not be ignored or pushed to the back."

I never quite understood what Mum was talking about. It was impossible to ignore that woman. The years might have taken a toll on her height and her hearing, but not on her looks or bearing. Her pale skin was completely without wrinkles, as she had avoided the harsh Australian sun since first arriving in Australia at the age of nineteen. She got burnt once and never ventured into the sun again. Her figure was still trim and her posture perfect—the result of thirty years of weekly yoga classes.

"Stand up straight! Shoulders back!" she would always nag me. "It will make your tummy look smaller."

I always ignored the implied insult and said "Yes, *Mother*". I always complied, but with just a touch of civil disobedience. She hated it when I called her "Mother". Mum would never leave the house without lipstick and earrings, and every item of her dark-coloured clothing was carefully selected to enhance her figure and perfectly coiffed red hair.

Now in her mid-seventies, Mum comes into the shop for a half-day, twice a week. She loves keeping up with the latest styles and chatting to the customers. Unlike most women, I have never lied about my age. I was fortunate to have inherited Mum's perfect skin, so no one believes that I am in my early fifties. Then, when I introduce my mum, they look at her with added disbelief—they often think that we're sisters. Because I can't help myself (I love teasing her!), I always remark how wonderful she looks for being ninety-four. Mum's throwing arm is still working perfectly, I'm happy to say! However, her aim has never been good and I'm still faster than she is.

Of course, I would never ever dare to say any such thing if the customer were a man. You see, Mum still loves to flirt. Young men, old men—it makes no difference. She lowers her head and bats her eyelashes at them at them, throwing her shoulders back and pushing her still-full breasts forward. She smiles coquettishly at every man who walks through the door as she offers to help them find that perfect gift. After forty years together, my stepfather is still left speechless when she works her wiles on him. She may be a reluctant senior, but she is definitely a sexy one!

Lingerie manufacturers have a preconceived idea of what women want to wear. Teenagers want to wear stripes and spots in bright colours and pyjamas with teddy bears on them. Once you leave puberty, you become either a slut or are in need of ugly beige support garments that are meant to torture any semblance of a curve into a seamless lump. Motherhood often means—well, we know you've had sex once, and that will be enough of that for you. Post-baby it's just ugliness and practicality as you have lost your identity as a woman. Now you are just a milk-producing, nappy-changing mound of flesh that once had form, which is now too loose to be of any use to anyone but your baby. Then the kids grow up—you go back to work, and as you are now "a woman of a certain age", you want to look tidy and attractive but not overtly sexy. A body is there to be covered and concealed but not enhanced. Then, when you're a "senior", it becomes a neck to knee prospect—arms are too flabby, legs too wobbly and the décolletage … well, how did that get so wrinkly? Better cover up. Obviously, no right-thinking woman above the age of sixty is having sex, so why wear anything sexy? And the manufacturers provide nothing appropriate other than pale pink and pale blue nighties and fluffy dressing gowns. After all, the only priority for the mature woman is to be warm and covered. She obviously doesn't care anymore, so why bother to supply her with anything that might awaken a long-forgotten memory of when she was young and her body gave her pleasure?

I have certain rules for my shop. I only stock garments that make a woman feel wonderful, grown up and sophisticated. There are certain things that I will not sell to certain ages. Young ladies under the age of eighteen should not wear see-through push-up bras. If a teenager comes in and asks for something like that, I tell her to return with her mother and then we can discuss it. Conversely, after a certain age, women look ridiculous in frilly babydolls. They just can't carry it off—unless they've had a request for a 1970s air-hostess look; then let the games begin!

There are women who are destined to love once and once only. There are women who will love many times. And then there are women who never stop having lovers. Beatrice was definitely one of the latter.

I could tell that she was going to be spectacular from the moment she set foot in my store. This was not a woman who entered a room quietly—no, not her. Tall and full figured, she made an entrance like a queen in an opera— "Everyone, look at me; I have something to say"—and sure enough, all eyes would be on her without the need to say a word. It almost seemed like she should have her own soundtrack to accompany her wherever she went!

When she first came in, she was wearing tailored black trousers and a matching skivvy; over the top she wore a long, loose, multicoloured burnout velvet coat lined with red satin, with about a dozen long gold chains of different lengths around her neck. Her long grey hair was styled into a glamorous French twist. A velvet pillbox hat that matched her coat was perched on her head at a rakish angle. Her eyes were pale green and lightly lined in kohl. Her lips, however, were full and emphasised with bright red lipstick. She had a wooden walking stick with a big green jewel on top which she used for dramatic effect rather than support; she banged it on the ground with each step. She pulled herself up to her full height—about six inches taller than me—and tapped her walking stick on the ground to make sure that everyone in the shop was paying attention.

After a moment's pause for effect, she announced for all to hear, in an imperious, well-modulated voice, "I am about to embark on an affair, and I need a corset".

Now, she wasn't talking about a girdle; she wanted a strapless, boned, black lace corset with matching briefs and stockings—a merry widow! This was most unusual. Not that she was having an affair or that she wanted a corset—it was the fact that she made sure to inform anyone in hearing distance. There were three other ladies in the store at the time browsing through the racks, and I was helping one of them with sizing for a camisole. Generally, when a lady walks into the shop and is about to have an encounter, they tend to be a little shy and discreet. They usually don't want any help initially, but I can always tell what's going on by the first thing they touch! (It's most often red.) I have a very romantic soul; I just love hearing about how people met, and there is nothing more pleasurable in my store than helping a lady to plan a seduction. It's not too difficult to get women to open up to me after they realise this, but it is always a private and intimate conversation. Not like this one!

When Beatrice was sure that all four of us were paying her the appropriate amount of attention, she continued with her story.

She had noticed him at a fundraiser for the local theatre group; she was one of the founding members and principal actress, but since good parts for ladies of a certain age were not common, lately she had had to make do with being cast as Mother or, G-d forbid, Grandmother. "If only I could sing," she said, "I could find plenty of parts in musicals, but I'm completely tone deaf".

Though in her early eighties, she knew she had weathered the years well. "Posture, ladies," she announced to us, her fascinated audience. "Stand up straight. It takes years off you!" I slowly pushed my shoulders back and grew an inch, and I noticed that the others did, too. We didn't want to earn her disapproval!

She continued to regale her entranced audience with her life history. All of her many husbands and lovers over the years were now dead, and she had just about given up on the idea of finding another dalliance—although there would always be admirers. She batted her eyelids demurely as she continued. She knew how to use her eyes and body to let a man know that he was desired and that if he played his cards right, he just might have a chance of a night of bliss with her. However, all of the men Beatrice met now were too old and decrepit for her. And they were all too short—how could she look up to a man if she, well, couldn't look up to him? When she was younger, this was not so much of an issue, especially if he was wealthy and bought her roses—preferably yellow, to match her blonde hair. And imagine how his stature grew if he was only five feet tall but bought her diamonds! But now that she was more mature, Beatrice had become more discerning and felt that she was not going to waste her time and affections on just anyone. He must tick every box on her extensive list, or he would just be a time waster—and there wasn't that much time left.

Beatrice had made discreet inquiries about him through her friends in the theatre. It turned out that he had noticed her, too. He had seen her in one of her plays and was intrigued. He came to the fundraiser in the hope of having a word with her and was thrilled to hear that she had noticed him as well. He was an ex-army captain fifteen years her junior. He was married; however, his wife had dementia and had been in a nursing home for a number of years just staring at the ceiling. Although he was devoted to her and visited her daily, there was nothing he could do other than get on with his life the best he could, and theatre had always been a passion. The captain knew little about Beatrice's personal life beyond her bio in the play program—which, in the best tradition of the theatre, had left her age as an enigma. She, of course, had no intentions of enlightening him. She was charmed by his deep voice and perfect grammar, as well as his excellent posture, and they agreed to meet.

He picked her up for their rendezvous dressed in an immaculate navy pinstriped suit and bearing a beautiful posy of miniature yellow roses. He was about six inches taller than her, and she was smitten. They met twice more for intimate dinners in dark, candlelit restaurants, where they would discuss theatre and life and loves and touch hands "accidentally" at every opportunity. Sparks flew, and soon the time came to consummate their relationship. He, of course, could not invite her back to his home;

they thought it inappropriate under the circumstances. Her place was also out of the question, as it would need a major tidy up as well as judicious removing of certain framed theatre reviews from the walls lest they give away her real age. He booked a room in an elegant boutique hotel in The Rocks area of Sydney where they were unlikely to run into any of his friends.

"People always have an opinion and don't mind sharing it," he told her. His wife hadn't said a word for five years and didn't know who he was; however, there would always be those who would judge. He just wanted to enjoy Beatrice's company without prying eyes.

I had been given my instructions and so set about finding her the perfect garment. I managed to talk her out of the regular boned corsets. The boning was made of either flexible plastic or soft metal; they always looked fine as long as they weren't too firm, in which case the boning would kink. Corsets are also somewhat uncomfortable; the bones can stick into you and restrict movement, and if you intend to roll around in bed that can be a bit of a hindrance. Steel-boned corsets are very rigid, and although they look fabulous, they make it difficult to breathe—which is hardly conducive to vigorous lovemaking! I also mentioned to her that corsets can be difficult to put on by yourself, as the hooks are in the back, meaning you have to close them in the front and then twist the garment around. I was almost hoping that she would tell me that she had a dresser to help her prepare!

She wasn't happy with the change in plans until I mentioned her rolling around in bed, and then her eyes lit up. We settled on a black hip-length, stretch-satin waist-cincher that opened in the front, with a black lace bra that had diamantes sewn into the straps. I found some black and red lace-top stockings; which she said would match perfectly with her black kitten heel mules trimmed with red maribou feathers. I then found a full-length silk chiffon robe with lace trim to go over the top so she could make an entrance and then slowly disrobe to candlelight and Frank Sinatra.

The affair continued for about six months, during which time she would come in and buy looser and looser garments. Rolling around on the bed was definitely easier in silk than in full regalia. However, she seemed to wear him out and he finally ended it—citing exhaustion from caring for both his wife's needs and Beatrice's. To tell the truth, she seemed relieved when she told me. She didn't have the heart to tell him that he was boring her with all his talk about his wife's condition and not enough talk about her magnificence.

"A woman needs to be both loved and adored," she said with a touch of melancholy, "and I for one was never going to be the supporting act."

I heard she died about six months after that, suffering a massive heart attack on stage in rehearsal for a local production of *The Vagina Monologues*.

Chapter 13

Girl talk

Men come into my shop for all sorts of reasons. Some are looking for a gift for their wife or girlfriend—or both. Some just like to browse seeking insight into the female mystique. Some come in looking for salvation—their marriages have become a bit boring and they're looking for a way to spice it up. Most are respectful, but every now and then a particularly sleazy type will see how far he can push the envelope. Just recently, a particularly disgusting fellow waltzed into the shop, picked up a very provocative lace body stocking, shook it under a customer's nose and asked her to model it for him. I quickly got between them and firmly told him to leave. One look at my face and he knew I meant business. I wasn't sure if he'd lost a bet or was just naturally creepy, but I wasn't taking any chances. Luckily, those types of incidents are few and far between.

By the time my shop had been operating for about eighteen months, I had begun to build up a lovely clientele of local customers and people who worked in the area. I was getting a reputation as someone who could give good advice.

On this particular day, I noticed a fellow hanging around outside the shop. He was in his mid-thirties—pleasant looking and clean shaven, with short brown hair and dressed in jeans and a button-down shirt. He seemed very tentative about entering a ladies' underwear shop. Looking for an excuse to talk to him without scaring him away, I grabbed a kettle from the kitchen so I could refill the water bowl I keep at the shop door for the local dogs. I smiled at him and said "Hi" as I poured water into the bowl.

He seemed a bit embarrassed—as if I had caught him peeking at forbidden things. "Can I come in and look?" he asked.

"Of course," I said. "If you need any help, just let me know."

He came in and walked around the racks with his hands firmly at his side—careful not to knock anything over. He stopped in front of some pretty pink bras and reached up as if to touch them, but then quickly returned his hand to his side. I wasn't getting any vibe from him that he wanted to chat or was looking for any suggestions. He then went to a rack and stopped at the section with cotton shortie pyjamas, the ones in a white and pink floral with a matching robe. He smiled shyly at me, said "Thank you" and made a quick exit.

I didn't think about him again until he came in a few weeks later. He went to the same two racks but this time asked for some prices. He was still careful not to touch anything; and he seemed to avert his eyes from a lot of the sexier things. I asked if he knew what sizes he was looking for, and he looked completely perplexed— as if I had asked him to explain Einstein's theory of relativity. He said he would have to check and left.

There was something unusual about him, but —I couldn't quite put my finger on it. Over the years men have asked me all sorts of weird and wonderful questions about lingerie items, for all kinds of reasons. I've had cross-dressers through the shop who have never indulged in their fetish and needed help in understanding what goes where, so to speak. They are often quite embarrassed to start with, but once they realise that my shop is a judgement-free zone, they open up to me. There are men who like their wives or girlfriends to look like virgins and those who like them to look like vixens. Anything goes! I do not sell any fantasy costumes or bondage gear, but every year around the time of the Sleaze Ball—that uniquely Sydney bacchanalia that cohabits with the Gay Mardi Gras—I'm inundated with straight men looking for a corset and fishnet stockings. They're always very quick to tell me that they are straight, that it's just fancy dress.

This man, however, did not seem to be doing anything other than trying to figure something out.

We were coming up to Mother's Day. There were lots of fellows coming into the shop to buy gifts for their wives or mothers; either from themselves or on behalf of their children to give to their mums. Feminine pyjama sets with matching robes were a bestselling item that year.

The day before Mother's Day, he came into the shop again. Walking shyly behind him was a pretty, slender young girl with long blonde hair pulled back in a ponytail. She seemed to be in her early teens but was quite well developed. She had grabbed a fistful of his sweatshirt and was holding on to it for dear life. She appeared quite embarrassed.

"Okay," I thought. "He's looking for a present for his wife." I smiled at him and asked if he needed any help.

"Wait here a minute, sweetheart." He smiled at his daughter as he gently disengaged her hand from his top and came over to talk to me privately.

"I need help," he explained quietly. He looked directly at me; he appeared somewhat perplexed and out of his depth. "This is my daughter. My wife died many years ago and it's just us now. We've managed quite well up till now, the two of us. But there are no women in my family. I try to be both mum and dad to her—but now she needs a bra and I haven't got a clue where to start."

Well, that explained so much! The father/daughter relationship is always special. From the moment you understand that men and women are different, he will be the strongest person you know. He will be your protector and hero, and when he carries you high on his shoulders, you know you are queen of the world and there is nothing and no-one who can hurt you. His strength, authority and wisdom make you feel comforted and safe. You also learn how to flirt from batting your eyelashes at him when you want something, and kissing daddy on the cheek will be your first kiss.

However, there are times when a girl just needs her mum, and this was one of those moments. Your first bra is a time of celebration—you are becoming a woman, and you don't have to shove oranges into your bikini top any more to pretend that you are one. But the reality of growing breasts can be a bit frightening. Where did they come from? Why weren't they there before? Why do they bounce around so much? Why is one bigger than the other? Am I going to die? Why do they hurt? Why am I so big/small/pointy/round? WHY IS/ISN'T THIS HAPPENING TO ME?

It's also a time of loss. You know that life will never be the same again. Dressing won't be as simple. Running won't be either. Going to the beach will leave you equally embarrassed and envious. Mine seemed to grow overnight when I was twelve. I have photos taken a month apart where I am quite flat-chested in one, still a girl, and then *kaboom*—I'm a D-cup and look very much like a woman. I even remember the moment that I realised something was happening. I woke up one morning and looked down, and there they were! What a shock it was! I ran out of the bedroom in tears, straight into my mother's arms. "Does this mean I am going to have big boobies like—" I was going to say "you", but I didn't want to offend her. "—like Aunty Golda?" And I wailed and wailed. I always thought my mother and her sisters were beautiful, but those breasts seemed enormous and I sure as buggery didn't want them. Well, my mum thought this was the funniest thing she had ever heard and couldn't stop laughing. It was a fabulous dinner conversation topic for months afterwards with all her girlfriends.

I got over my tears and the initial shock, though, and we went to get a bra. I still remember what it looked like—ivory moulded lace with a little pink bow in the centre. There was a lot of unwanted attention at school, as I was the first one to grow breasts. The boys liked to stare and snap my bra strap, and the girls were either jealous or happy that this hadn't yet happened to them. None of it really bothered me in the end. They were just a part of me, and that was that. The only difficulty was not being able to sleep on my tummy, and playing sport turned out to be problematic, as this was before the days of good sports bras. I would bounce both the basketball and me all over the court. I developed a method of dribbling the ball with my right hand, with my left arm crossed over in front of me to hold everything in place—somewhat ungainly, but effective.

"What's your name, sweetheart?" I asked as I ushered the young lady into the change room and took a quick measurement.

"Annie," she answered shyly.

I told her not to be embarrassed in front of me—that I had seen more boobs than she'd had hot dinners. However, I told her, I had to check the fit, and there was only one way to do it. If it would make her more comfortable, I said, I could take my top off, too. She giggled at the thought of that. First thing, however, before she got undressed, I wanted to make sure that she was ready to wear a bra. She looked like she needed one, but some girls are forced into them way too early and are emotionally unready for their first step into being a woman. I asked her to jump up and down. She looked unsure, so I jumped up and down to show her what I meant. My big boobs jumped with me but landed a second after I did. I laughed and said, "Did you see that? I almost gave myself a black eye. Now, let's see how much you move when you jump". She jumped up and down a few times, and there was enough movement there for her to feel uncomfortable. "Are you happy with that," I asked, "or would you like to have something on to stop them moving around too much? It's up to you". She said she felt self-conscious when they moved, so yes, she would like something to hold them in place.

I brought her the bra her father had looked at originally and a few others as well, all the time cracking jokes with her and her father so that she felt at ease and this would be a good memory for her. We found two bras that she liked and matched some pretty panties to them, as well as a nice PJ set that was a little more grown up than the teddy bear print she usually wore. After all, she was now well on her way to becoming a woman. I also gave her a little pep talk about what is normal. Young girls are bombarded with so many images of photoshopped, surgically-enhanced bodies that they have no idea how they are meant to look. The important thing to know is that whatever size and shape they are, they are absolutely perfect and completely normal. No amount of dieting or exercise will change what they are genetically meant to be. So, if that's the case, then you *must* be perfect. The exciting part is watching the canvas change over the years.

"You should make friends with your boobs," I told her. "Give them names. Mine are called 'Mini' and 'Maxi' because one is bigger than the other".

Annie thought that was hilarious. She looked thoughtful for a moment and then announced, "I am going to call mine 'Eeny Meeny' and 'Miny Moe'".

"Which one is which?" I asked.

"What? Can't you tell?" she asked mischievously.

I told Annie to leave one of the bras on, get dressed and then come out and show her dad how grown up she looked.

I left her to it and went to chat with her father. He told me his name was Ben and he thanked me for helping him. Annie was growing up so fast, and as each day passed, she was looking more and more like her mother. It brought him so much joy, but it made the loss of his wife even more painful—especially in moments like these.

After about ten minutes, Annie finally made her appearance. She had dressed with extra care, tucking her loose T-shirt into her jeans so her shape was more prominent and changed her hair from a pony tail to a bun at the top of her head. She walked out of the change room, standing tall and with her shoulders back; she looked very proud of herself and her new figure. I watched Ben as she appeared, he was so transfixed by her that he forgot to blink.

"I thought you were your mum," he stammered after a moment, his voice catching in his throat as he held back the tears.

Annie smiled proudly, recognising the compliment, and then ran into her father's arms for a hug. The safest and best place in the world.

Her father seemed so relieved to have this problem fixed. There would be many more things he would have to cope with, but getting this first big one out of the way was a great help. As they were leaving, Annie reached up and gave him a gentle kiss on the cheek, saying, "Thanks, Dad."

They have been coming back twice a year ever since for new bras, always around the same time—in May for Mother's Day and in September for Father's Day.

Postscript

Annie is all grown up now and doesn't need her father to accompany her for bras anymore. He remarried a lovely lady called Julia. She and Annie look nothing alike, but the bond between them is obvious: Julia treats Annie like her daughter.

Last year, Annie brought her to the shop to introduce me to her. She was petite and slender with large, laughing brown eyes, a ready smile and long, dark, curly hair. Annie introduced me to Julia as "Maxi" and "Mini".

Julia smiled knowingly and said, "Hi! Lovely to meet you finally. 'Eeny Meeny—Miny Moe' has told me so much about you. I'm 'Itsy' and 'Bitsy'!"

Chapter 14

Circus

It felt like the circus had come to town. That was all I could make of this day. Most of the time I have regular customers who come in and have a fitting and a chat and are on their way without much fuss. Just regular ladies with regular needs. Lost some weight and need to be resized; bought a new dress and need a good slip to go under it; going away for the weekend and need some new PJs— just normal stuff. This day was different.

It was quiet to start with. I opened the shop at 10.30 in the morning, and it was already 1.00 pm; there had been a couple of lookers-in, but no one really interested in buying today. But that's retail. You never know who is going to come in and when. I am very happy with my own company and can keep myself occupied without too much fuss. There is always unpacking to do or rearranging or tidying. And if I don't feel like doing any of that, I like to knit jumpers that I sell in the shop—pretty, lacy styles that suit the lingerie. Some days I can get to work and there are people waiting for me, while on others, no-one will walk in for hours and nothing really happens till I want to close. Every day is a mystery.

This particular day I was sitting, knitting away for an order I had taken from a customer. It was for a huge lace shawl in six different yarns in shades of teal to go over a silk pyjama set instead of a robe. I was concentrating on a tricky section where the yarns had to change over without appearing to do so when I looked up—and there she was, standing in all her botoxed glory.

She was blonde and slender and, as far as I could tell, in her mid-thirties. Her face was like a mask—high eyebrows, wide open and heavily made-up eyes with long fake eyelashes, upturned nose, pumped up cheeks and pumped up lips she couldn't control. When she started talking, they seemed to be moving out of sync with the words—kind of like a badly dubbed Godzilla movie.

"Chello. Are you Polina? My nem is Natasha. My friend told me to come. I ched boobs done and need new bra." The accent was Russian and very guttural.

Normally when someone comes in, the first thing I do is check out the state of their boobs—occupational hazard, I guess. I look to see if they're wearing a good bra or need resizing. I check their posture and if their tops are fitting well or could be improved by better cleavage. It has become second nature to me. I have to consciously make myself not do this out in public or I would spend half my time shaking my head from side to side in despair. I am, of course, by no means perfect and have had my own bra disasters over the years (I've actually 'busted' a bra open with a huge sneeze!). However, in this case I couldn't stop staring at her face. She could have stepped out of Madame Tussauds. Everything was frozen except for those lips. They kept twitching even when she stopped talking.

"No problem," I said. "Why don't you pop into the change room and I will see what you need?"

I gave her a few minutes to undress and then went over for a look. She was about a 32F–FF, so I brought over a selection of bras.

"No—this is wrong," she said. "I am D-cup. I ask doctor for D-cup and I am D-cup."

Cup size is determined by a number of different factors. Volume is one, but so is how much percentage of the chest wall is taken up by breast tissue. You can be almost flat chested, but if your breasts start under your arm you will need a bigger cup size. The art is then finding the perfect style for your shape. Most breast implants measure up a lot bigger than intended. The surgeons only understand how many cc's are going in—not how to fit a bra. She may have asked for D-cups, but what she ended up with were at least F-cups, as the implants were placed quite wide apart.

I tried to explain this to her. I couldn't tell if she understood or not as her face held no expression. She did blink a couple of times, though, so that was something. I handed her a pretty white lace bra and told her to try it on.

I stepped away to let her get changed, and after a few minutes I hear "I'm ready now." I opened the curtain and she was wearing the bra; of course, it was a perfect fit, but she didn't like the effect.

"I am not cheppy. I vant boobs togeder." She tried to push them closer to each other to show me what she wanted, but they wouldn't budge. The implants were set too far apart and were hard as rocks. It was like they were made of cement. There was a gap of over an inch between them.

We tried on some Wonderbra plunge bras that normally create magnificent cleavage—but not on these rocks. What the surgeon had set asunder, no mere bra could bring together. Halter-neck bras made no difference. Extra side padding just made her breasts look wider. We were at it for about an hour, and I could see she was getting frustrated. She was examining herself from every angle possible in the mirrors, looking for some strangely perceived idea of perfection. If her forehead hadn't been botoxed, I'm sure she would have been frowning.

On all the mirrors in the change rooms I have placed a sign that says:

REFLECTIONS IN THIS MIRROR MAY BE 'DISTORTED' BY SOCIALLY ACCEPTED IDEAS OF BEAUTY
The management

I asked her to read the sign. She shook her head. It made no difference.

"I vont to look sexy. Togeder, boobs look sexy. Apart—not sexy. Just big, like cow."

"Aww, honey—being sexy has nothing to do with the size of your boobs. It's all about how you feel inside and how you move," came a high-pitched, squeaky voice.

I turned around to see who spoken, and there she was—a dwarf on a scooter.

She was no more than three feet tall—pretty face, long dark hair and wearing a pink dress and running shoes. She was hanging on to a child's scooter for balance and was half riding, half pushing it around the shop.

"My boyfriend thinks I am the sexiest thing on three wheels and all I have to do is wink at him."

Natasha wasn't impressed. "Yes, but boobs should be togeder for good shape. Dis is vot sexy is, no?"

"No—sexy is how you feel inside," she said. "It's something that comes from within. It's got nothing to do with how you look. I dance at Burlesque bars and believe me—when I do this move, they all stand and applaud." She pulled herself up and sashayed across the shop, wiggling her hips—all the time holding on to the scooter. Then she slowly turned around and started shimmying; it started with her shoulders slowly twirling back and forwards, one after the other. Her breasts followed suit, and soon they took on a life of their own as they started moving in circles but in opposite directions. Her arms were spread out wide, her head was thrown

114

back in joy—everything was gyrating, till I thought she would fall over. She finally slowed down, lowered her head at an angle and gave us an extravagant wink! I was about to yell "Brava" when she curtsied prettily and said, "Now that's sexy."

"No—sexy is boobs togeder." Natasha pouted and tried again to push them in, apparently oblivious to the spectacular show that we had just experienced.

It turned out the other woman's name was Monique, and she danced in clubs all around Australia. I asked if I could help her with anything; her boyfriend had requested a see-through nightie. I found her a sheer black camisole that reached her knees, which she bought.

Natasha was getting annoyed that we weren't paying enough attention to her problem. I agreed with Monique that you can't buy sexy from a doctor's office. It is something you feel. Sophia Loren said, "Sex appeal is 50% what you've got and 50% what people think you've got". The surgeon could have stuck those implants so close together that they overlapped, but if you ain't got it, you ain't got it!

"But chow can I shake like you if boobs don't go togeder?" Natasha asked.

Monique started moving her shoulders to demonstrate, all the time holding on to her scooter. She then held on to her breasts on either side and started to clap them together. Natasha tried, but she had boulders cemented to her chest and nothing moved—although I thought I saw a slight wrinkle try and bust through the skin on her brow as she concentrated. Poor Natasha. She really had no idea.

By this point I had reached the edge—it took every ounce of strength I had to maintain my professional demeanour and not burst out laughing. I felt like I was in that scene in Monty Python's *Life of Brian* when the centurion tries not to laugh at Biggus Dickus. I bit my lip; stuck my fingernails into my hand; thought of root canal therapy—anything to keep me from cracking up. Monique was prancing around the shop—and Natasha was trying to copy her. Monique was full of *joie de vivre*. Natasha was full of doubts. Monique was lithe and graceful. Natasha was a robot. I was beginning to think that maybe this was some kind of set-up ... and I started looking for the hidden cameras.

After about another fifteen minutes of carrying on, Monique left.

"Enough of this game," she drawled. "I got me a date with my boyfriend and a bottle of wine."

Natasha shrugged her shoulders—one last failed attempt at a shimmy. She purchased the Wonder Bra, sighed a sad little sigh and also left.

Just in time—I couldn't hold it in any more. I laughed myself silly as I tidied up after them.

My grandmother used to say that it takes all kinds to make up a world. I just wasn't expecting to meet those two at the same time. It was like the circus had come to town and pitched its tent in my shop.

"What next?" I thought.

Then the one-legged, eyepatch-wearing transvestite walked in...

Chapter 15

A three-hug day

Mum got Alzheimer's and died.

There, I've said it. Five straightforward words but if only it was that simple. It wasn't. It was two years of hell. Strange symptoms started to appear. She refused to wear her hearing aid. Always a vain woman who fought against ageism with a passion, she wouldn't wear it because, in her mind, hearing loss was an old person's problem and every time she looked in the mirror, she still saw a young woman with beautiful unlined skin. So, in her opinion, if she wasn't old, she couldn't have a hearing problem and there was definitely no need for that ridiculous hearing aid. No amount of cajoling or yelling would change her mind. As far as she was concerned the phones were broken and everybody mumbled.

Then she fell over and broke her hip. Her bones were very strong, and she had no signs of arthritis or skeletal degeneration. It was just a bad fall on some wet leaves. The hip replacement operation was a success as far as the surgeon was concerned but we noticed something else. It was as if the anaesthesia never quite left her brain. She seemed a little vague and not quite as "with it" as she usually was.

Swearing was a new symptom that was hard to ignore. Mum never swore in her life. Ladies never used profane language and she was a lady. The first "FUCK YOU" she threw at me when I was five minutes late picking her up shocked me. Then there were ten more, one after the other like machine guns firing at my heart. I didn't know whether to laugh or cry. All I could think to say was "MUM!" She apologised, but over the course of the evening she repeated it many times before graduating to "FUCK A POO POO". The filters were clearly off and she was obviously not aware of what she was saying.

Then she forgot how to walk, and we had to put her in a home because my stepfather could no longer look after her.

She was very well taken care of and she knew who I was, but when I asked her who I was she would smile and say "Mary Smith". When pushed she would say that I was her daughter. I so desperately wanted her to say my name but when I asked her "which one" she said, "the good one". I suppose I was happy with that. Mum also began telling me over and over that she loved me. She was never very forthcoming with words of affection, so I guess this change was a good thing.

She was still very beautiful and the nurses at the home would dye her hair red, paint her nails and she wore all her jewellery and make-up every day. All the nursing staff would comment on how much I looked like her. One day, the most poignant thing happened. I was walking down the aisle to mum's room and one of the nurses saw me from a distance and thought that I was mum and that it was a miracle and that mum was up and walking again. When the nurse told me this, I wish she hadn't. It broke my heart.

Mum died and we buried her. Somehow, I managed to write and give a 20-minute eulogy at the service which was attended by many friends and family.

Then I went home and stood in front of the mirror and looked at my reflection. However. the only one looking back at me was mum.

I cried myself to sleep.

Hug number one

I closed the shop for a couple of days and spent my days on ferries, roaming Sydney Harbour. There is something so restorative about being on the water. I had hoped for a few more days to myself, but my staff member abruptly quit, and I had to bite the bullet and go back to work. My first few days passed in a bit of a blur but then the fog lifted, and I reconnected with my shop and all of my lovely customers. I started to feel somewhat restored.

Regulars were dropping in to check up on me. They weren't used to seeing the shop closed as we open seven days a week. That's when HUG NUMBER ONE came in.

She was quite a busty girl. Young and pretty and in awe of the range of bras and sizes in the shop. She told me that every bra buying experience she had would always end in tears. "You're too big—this is the best you can expect," they would say as they handed her an ugly beige sling. It left her feeling fat and ugly when she was actually pretty and slim, but with a big bust. A legacy from her father's side she explained.

I took a quick measurement and then ushered her into the change room. I handed her a red and black lace balconette bra with a matching G-string, as well as a sheer black lace plunge bra.

"Are *these* for me?" she asked incredulously.

"Yes! Try on the red one first," I replied.

I left her to disrobe and then suddenly I heard the sound of laughter coming from the change room. "Oh no," I thought to myself. "I got it wrong."

I went to check, and she was standing in front of the mirror wearing the bra with the biggest grin on her face. The bra fit her well and she was ecstatic. She'd never thought that she would ever be able to wear anything so pretty and fashionable.

She ended up taking four bras sets as well as a strapless bra. Her first ever.

As she left, she asked if she could give me a hug because this was the first bra buying experience that actually made her feel happy. A common or garden variety of hug but lovely just the same.

Hug number two

About an hour later a mother and daughter came in together searching for something for the daughter's wedding night. They obviously got on very well and were giggling away as they were talking about how excited they were for the wedding. The daughter, Ruth, was a little taller than her mother but they looked very much alike with slender figures, long blonde hair and piercing pale blue eyes. Ruth had been planning her wedding since she was a little girl. Somebody had once remarked that she looked just like Princess Di as a little girl, and after looking her up Ruth became obsessed by the princess in her wedding dress with the bridesmaids and horse-drawn carriage. She wanted the same kind of fairytale wedding and her dress was very like Princess Di's, but with a little less flounce and a little more cleavage. She would arrive at the church in a horse-drawn carriage and she had a veil designed with a tiara just like Princess Di's tiara, but of course the diamonds wouldn't be real.

That was where the resemblance to Princess Di ended.

"So, who do you want to be on your wedding night?" I asked. "A virgin or a vixen?"

Both mother and daughter burst out laughing.

"She hasn't been a virgin for a long time. That ship has definitely sailed!" her mother smirked.

Ruth shrugged her shoulders and smiled. "I always fancied one of those corsets with stockings that you see in the movies. I think they're very sexy. I haven't decided if I want a black one or an ivory one like my dress."

I asked what underwear she was wearing under her dress. She said that her dress had heavy boning all through the bodice and she just needed some knickers and maybe a suspender belt and stockings in ivory.

"May I make a suggestion?" I asked. "Your wedding day is going to start very early and finish late. It's tiring. And you will be wearing a heavy wedding dress with full boning. The last thing that you will want to do is take off that dress and put on some more boning with a corset. I know you want to mark the occasion of your wedding night, and who doesn't, but there is a more comfortable way to do it."

I had just received a range from the USA of honeymoon nighties and robes. All in ivory and all exquisite. In Australia, the best I could find was in plain silk and maybe a camisole/French knicker set with a lace insert, but that was it. Nothing glamorous or memorable at all about the styling.

I pulled out a long ivory satin nightgown (this was definitely not a "nightie") with lace cups embroidered with pearls and sequins, a low back and thigh-high side-splits. The matching robe was in satin with full lace sleeves edged in the matching pearls and sequins. It was exquisite.

Ruth just stared and her mother could say nothing other than, "Oh my!"

"Well," I said. "If this is your reaction, can you imagine your future husband's reaction when he sees you in this."

Ruth took the hanger from my hand and walked off to the change room. I continued showing her mum a few other items from the range. There were shorter chemises with the same pearl and sequin embellishments, camisole and knicker sets and babydolls with chiffon draped over the cups. After a few minutes Ruth stepped out of the change room wearing the set with the robe closed. She walked up to us with a huge grin on her face, and then slowly undid the satin belt from the robe and let it fall off her shoulders as she walked back to the change room. She knew she looked spectacular, and her future husband was going to love it.

She got changed, came out and placed the set on the table. She asked if she could take it on the hanger and I went to the back of the shop to find some plastic to place over it so she could carry it to their car without anything staining it. When I came back, mother and daughter were arguing about who was going to pay. Ruth insisted that her mother had done enough for her already, but her mother was not to be dissuaded. It was her absolute pleasure to make her daughter's wedding day as perfect as she could.

"Can I give you a couple of words of advice from an old married woman who's worked with lingerie to a young bride?" I asked. Ruth nodded and her mother looked intrigued, wondering what on earth I was going to say.

"Keep wearing lingerie. Once the honeymoon is over and you come back home and start your married life together it's easy to become complacent and comfortable and before you know it you are like best mates sitting on the couch and you're taking each other for granted. Keep the romance alive with lingerie. It's not about sex, but connection. You wear something fabulous and he looks at you and you look at him looking at you and you've connected. Never let that go."

"You are so right," her mother said. "Thank you for all your help. Do you mind if I give you a hug?"

I stood up and went around the table and she put her arms around me and before we could say "here comes the bride" Ruth joined in and we had a lovely three-way bear hug.

They left with Ruth holding her beautiful peignoir set carefully over her arm and her mother smiling in that knowing way that mother's get when they know that good things are going to happen to their children.

Hug number three

It was close to closing time and I was just reflecting upon the day it had been. Two lovely hugs along with several other customers with specific requests that I was able to help them with. A lady needing a seam-free G-string, someone else for a strapless bra and another with a very small bust who needed a bra with heavy padding in order to fill out the princess seams in her dress. Then a woman walked in.

She was petite with long dark hair, large black eyes, late-thirties and with an air of sadness about her. She said she needed a new bra as the one she had was no longer any good.

I took a quick measurement in my usual way—I asked her to turn around so I could feel how wide her back was. Then to turn to me and I put my second finger on either side of each breast so I could feel how wide her breast tissue was across her chest wall. This also tells me if one side is different to the other. I noticed that she was wearing a bra without a wire which can change the way a size presents—sometimes such bras press all the breast tissue flat. I also noticed that she had quite a puffy belly that was hidden under loose clothing.

I led her to the change room and asked what colour she wanted.

"I don't really care. Just something that fits that isn't the one that I'm wearing."

As she came in wearing dark clothing, I chose a couple of styles in black for her to try. I handed them to her and told her to tell me when she ready for me to check the size.

After a few minutes she calls out that she thinks it's okay, so I open the curtains to check. The fit seemed fine, but I realised that the bra that she had taken off was a maternity bra, and that she had only recently given birth.

"How does that feel?" I asked.

She said it felt comfortable and did I have the same thing in another colour.

I didn't, but I brought her a different style in a pretty honey colour. Not beige, but a lovely warm colour that matched her skin well. She handed me her maternity bra and asked me to throw it away.

"I don't need this," she stated blankly. "My baby died. Stillborn."

"I'm so sorry," was all I could think to say.

"I'll never have my baby—that was the tenth IVF and I can't do any more cycles."

She asked if she could leave the black one on and she would take both of them. She made herself busy getting dressed again and as I turned to leave to give her some privacy she continued talking.

"Do you know what the worst thing is?" I couldn't imagine

anything worse, so I let her talk. She obviously needed to say something out loud.

"On the day my daughter died—three weeks ago today—my mother was driving to the hospital to help me through the birth and she was killed by a drunk driver. They didn't tell me for two days and I barely noticed as I was given so many drugs after the …" She couldn't utter the words again.

I felt my heart break at her loss. I had been feeling so sorry for myself, but Mum was eighty-two and it was her time. I was in deep mourning, but it wasn't a tragedy. It was the way of the world. This was something else.

She came out wearing her new bra and with the other one in her hand which she wordlessly handed to me with her credit card. I took payment and wrapped the bra in red tissue, placed it in a black paper bag and handed it to her.

"Do you mind if I give you a hug?" I asked. I so wanted to take away her pain, even as I was struggling with my own. She nodded and I came around my desk and put my arms around her and held her close. She put her head on my shoulder and sobbed as she put her arms tentatively around me. In that moment I became her mother, and my mother, and every mother in the world who has ever held back their own emotions to comfort their child. I felt the strength of a million tears pouring out of me and into her. We held each other for a few minutes, and I could feel her slowly taking control of her emotions. She pulled back, nodded her head to me, mouthed a silent "thank you" to me and then turned around and walked out of the shop.

Chapter 16

Four colours

It's never the ones you think.

Some women walk in the door and I automatically think of a word or colour to describe them. It isn't necessarily because of what shade they're wearing or how they're dressed; it's more about the spirit that emanates from them. Their aura. Some women come into my shop with a sense of expectation, some a sense of dread; some are desperate, and some are joyous. There are women who are purple, red, vibrant floral…

This lady was blank. The first word that came to mind was …

Beige

She was in her mid-fifties, of middling height and average figure. Her hair was a shade of mousey blonde, not quite gold and not quite brown, with strands of grey running through it, cut in a short bob with a fringe. She wore absolutely no make-up—not even lip gloss. The frown lines around her mouth were quite pronounced, and it looked like she hadn't smiled in a long time.

Her eyes were a nondescript brown framed by old-fashioned, metal-rimmed glasses. She was wearing an ivory pair of slacks; on anyone else they'd be pants, but on her they were definitely slacks. She rounded off the look with a tucked in shirt to match, a slightly darker button-up cardigan and a pair of caramel loafers. She kind of looked like a vanilla cream biscuit. All her clothes seemed half a size too big, as if any suggestion of a body underneath might imply that she was a woman and therefore existed.

All I could think of was BEIGE.

I gave her a few minutes to look around the shop and then asked if she needed any help with sizes or had an item in mind that I could help her find. People's eyes usually go straight to what they're looking for, or else they ask if they can't find it. I can normally tell straight away if someone is after something for a hot date or is just in need of new things for the new season. But I was getting nothing from her. She was s total blank.

"No, thank you," she told me, her voice toneless and nondescript.

She continued to browse, getting closer to the red bras and suspender belts. I thought, "Here we go!" to myself as I waited for her face to screw up in distaste at such a blatant sexual display … but she approached them in the same manner as the rest of the shop.

She then asked if she could try on a black silk chemise. The slip was knee length; although very plain it was a well-cut classic piece that flattered just about every figure. I found her size and led her to the change room.

My change rooms are at the back of the shop and face each other. There's a navy curtain on each one, slightly transparent, so that I can see if someone needs help with sizes or hooks. No-one can see into the rooms but me, and I always supervise every fitting to make sure that each customer gets the perfect fit.

I asked her if the size was okay and if she needed me to adjust the shoulder straps to the correct length.

She said yes, please, so I opened the curtains and found her standing in front of the mirror, gazing at herself like she was looking at a stranger. The chemise was cut on the cross and flattered her figure beautifully, which was a lot curvier than her clothes suggested. Her breasts were full and firm and her figure was classic hourglass—narrow waist and shapely hips. As I adjusted the straps, she started talking.

"I went to a Catholic school," she said, her voice a flat monotone. "The nuns taught us to love Jesus and the church and to be good and obedient wives—to always put our husbands and family first, before anything else."

I didn't know where she was going with this; people often tell me things, but this seemed so out of the blue. She sounded like she was going over the words she was saying in her head first. She barely seemed to notice that I was there with her.

"I have always been a good wife," she continued.

I got the feeling that she didn't actually want to engage me in conversation, that she wasn't waiting in any way for a comment from me. I didn't know what to say, anyway. "That's nice" seemed so inane, but that was all that came to mind.

"I've brought up two sons who are now in their twenties," she said. "I've always been faithful to my husband and kept a clean home. I've cooked and cleaned and done the laundry and devoted myself to my family." She paused and then said, "However, I have just met a man…"

Now she had my attention. I looked up at her; she was still staring at herself in the mirror, but now there was a light in her eyes that hadn't been there before.

"He told me that all he wants from me is for me to go to his place, get undressed and lie in his bed with my legs open and waiting for him. Then he wants to hold me while I sleep."

Well, you could have knocked me over with a feather, but I remained calm, nodded and made agreeing sounds as I fussed around the straps of the chemise. Finally, she looked at me for the first time, with an intensity that was almost like a plea for understanding from an axe murderer.

"You see," she said, "my husband and my sons have Asperger's syndrome. I haven't had a hug in thirty years."

I always thought that I couldn't be shocked. I mean, after over thirty years in this business, you think you've heard it all. I don't approve of cheating, but that's me, and I can't tell anyone else what to do. Most people justify their infidelities in purely selfish terms, without any reference to morality or concern for anyone other than themselves. They're just having some fun; who will be hurt anyway? However, you can't judge anyone till you have walked a mile in their shoes—and this was different. Her eyes were pleading for understanding, and the hidden moral battle she must have been waging in her mind was biblical in nature. She was clearly going against everything she had been taught and believed in.

But a woman needs to be touched. A woman needs to be held. A woman needs to feel loved. I understood.

But after that revelation, she broke eye contact with me and went back to looking at herself in the mirror, so I finished with her straps and left the change room.

After about five minutes she emerged—back to beige with blank eyes. She placed the slip on my desk and silently handed me a credit card. I carefully wrapped the slip in red tissue, making sure not crease it, and placed it in a red carry bag.

She never said another word before leaving the shop, not even "Thank you" or "Goodbye".

I never saw her again, although I often thought of her and hoped that she had found the affection she so obviously craved and was able to enjoy it without guilt.

Baby pink

I had just received a large shipment of bras from the USA. Four big boxes with over 1,000 pieces inside. Even after all these years of owning my shop, I still get ridiculously excited when a new delivery comes in. It's like a present just for me as I open each box and ooh and aah over all the new styles. I've yet to feel blasé or bored by the prospect of each new season's fashions.

Excitement aside, there's a lot of work involved with unpacking this amount of stock and checking off each style to see that it's all been delivered as ordered. (I once was delivered a fuchsia and black polka dot corset instead of the plain black because they misread the colour code. Needless to say, it went back and was replaced with the correct colour. Fuchsia corsets would definitely not be a hot item in quiet suburban Crow's Nest!) I then have to price everything and find room on the racks, which can entail a lot of rearranging of stock.

I was so involved with what I was doing that particular day that I didn't notice her enter. I finally looked up and she was standing in the corner, looking shyly at the corsets. "Baby pink," I thought to myself. "Pale, sweet baby pink." She seemed so young and shy and out of place gazing at the sexy corsets.

"Can I help you with anything?" I asked.

She looked like she'd been caught doing something she shouldn't.

"Uh... Um... No... Thank you... No." She looked like she wanted to bolt out the door, but something was obviously keeping her in the shop. She looked about fourteen, but if she were to put some make-up on and a pair of heels, she could probably pass for fifteen. There was just something so very young and youthful about her. She was dressed in blue jeans and a white T-shirt with a seated pink poodle printed on it (it was very cute and I would've liked one for myself, but a black poodle of course). She hadn't lost her baby fat yet; she had a little paunch hanging over the top of her jeans and a medium size bust— about a C cup. Her hair was a pretty shade of dark, strawberry blonde, almost red, with eyes that were a striking shade of light green. Her skin was very pale, with a smattering of freckles over her nose, but her full cheeks were turning a bright shade of rose as she blushed furiously—obviously mortified at being caught looking at lingerie inappropriate for her age.

"Why don't you keep looking," I said, not wanting to compound her embarrassment, "and when you see something you like just give me a yell." I went back to my boxes and left her to browse. Rummaging through the box, I pulled out a pretty tea-rose satin bra with matching pink and apricot cross-dyed lace over the cups. It was heavily lined on the inside so as not to show nipples through the lace. I held it up. "This is the latest colour and high fashion for summer," I said. "Don't you think it's pretty?"

She looked at it and shook her head. She wouldn't look me in the eyes; she turned away and then inquired, "Does it come in red?"

"Red? No—not this season," I answered. "Maybe next year."

She moved to the rack that held all the red bras and picked one up. She wanted it in whatever her size was; she wasn't sure what that was, as she'd never been measured. I must have had a questioning expression on my face, because she insisted that she wanted a red bra just like the one she was showing me. Well, she'd happened to pick up a sheer mesh red bra with vertical seams and a booster pad that sat under the cup to give extra lift. It was incredibly sexy and sophisticated and obviously unsuitable for anyone below eighteen years of age.

This was such a delicate moment. She was so sweet and young and obviously in need of guidance. I wondered where her mother was. At no point did I want to discourage her, so I took a quick measurement and fibbed when I told her I didn't have that style in her size. I suggested something in pink instead.

"No, it has to be red," she insisted, almost defiantly.

"Are you trying to match a red dress?" I asked.

"No. I haven't got a boyfriend." She paused and then, with a huge effort to say it out loud, continued, "No-one even looks at me. I'm too fat and too ugly. I heard that boys like red bras so I thought if I got one then I might find a boyfriend."

It was clear she suddenly felt very humiliated, as she quickly turned away. I could see her shoulders heaving. She was weeping. No wonder her mother was nowhere in sight. This wasn't something that a very young lady could easily discuss with her mum. It's so much easier with a stranger.

"What's your name, sweetheart?" I asked her.

"Caitlyn," she sobbed through her tears.

How appropriate a name, I thought as I handed her a box of tissues and led her to sit on one of the red leather chairs behind my desk. She looked so young and innocent.

"Caitlyn," I said, "I'm going to tell you something, and it's very important that you pay attention. Any boy who is only interested in what colour bra you wear is not worth your attention. He's just a speck of dust on your sleeve that you can ignore or just flick away, like this." I made a disdainful face and pretended to brush something off my arm. She almost smiled. "The only boy who is worth anything is the one who thinks that your lovely green eyes are beautiful, that your smile is his joy, that you're the most wonderful thing in his life—regardless of what colour underwear you wear. He'll laugh at all your jokes and hang on every word you say. He's the one that looks inside and sees the *real* you and doesn't care about the clothes you wear or the shape of your body. You. Are. Beautiful. And. Perfect. Just. As. You. Are. And don't let anyone make you think otherwise. The thing to focus on is not whether you are what he wants—it's whether he's what *you* want. Sometimes it really is all about you."

I watched her breathe in and out as she took in what I had said—looking for a fault in the argument. She was so young and hadn't yet learnt to hide her emotions; her conflicted thoughts were clearly visible in the lines on her forehead. After a few moments, she threw her shoulders back and dabbed the tears from her eyes.

"Can I try on that pink bra, please?"

Red

Over the years I've noticed that people walk into my store in different ways. Some are tentative, others confident. There are those that are shy and overwhelmed and then those that walk in like they own the shop.

This lady was obviously on a mission. She strode into the store and didn't look around at all but came straight up to me. RED, I thought immediately. This lady is full of fire.

"I need something special," she stated confidently. "Something that says 'I'm in charge', but I don't want bondage or dominatrix. Nothing kinky. I just want to feel strong."

She had obviously thought about this a lot. Putting on lingerie can be like putting on a costume. We can, as women, be anyone we want to be with the right lingerie, from blushing bride to vivacious vixen, perfectly practical or flighty and frivolous. In front of me, obviously, stood a fabulous femme fatale.

She was in her mid-forties, with dark, wavy hair pulled back in a pony tail, olive skin and dark, flashing eyes. Her figure was curvy in the old-fashioned way; straight shoulders leading to a full bust, narrow waist flaring out to full hips. Her legs were long and lean, obviously fit and toned.

I took a quick measurement and chose a few different things for her to try on. She nixed all the pale colours straight away.

"Not those—I need something powerful." She picked up a purple retro-cami with an inbuilt bra and detachable suspender attachments. "Something like this is closer to what I need. Does it come in any other colours?"

"That one is just in the purple," I told her. "It has a matching G-string and I also happen to have black stockings with a purple seam and lace top that go perfectly." Most lingerie stores stock only basic colours—black or ivory, pink and maybe red. I've always loved colour and try and source unusual shades.

I left her to try it on and after a few minutes returned to check the fit. She was standing tall and straight in front of the mirror with her legs apart and her hands on her hips, staring at her reflection. A heavy, stylised crucifix on a heavy gold chain hung from her neck and fell into the cleavage created by the cami. She gently lifted it out, placed it over the top so she could see it and then returned her hands to her hips. Her toned arms were tense, and she almost looked like Wonder Woman—ready to take on the enemy.

"That'll do," she said firmly. "I think that will do just fine."

My curiosity was piqued, but I got the feeling that she didn't want to talk, so I just wrapped up her purchase, wished her well and watched her stride out of the store. Mission accomplished for that day.

A few weeks later, she was back. The fiery red aura was flaming brighter this time.

"That last set was good, but I need something else now. Even stronger."

This time I found her a very form-fitting, knee-length stretch-satin chemise in red, with clever stitching that enhanced her bust. It was cut very low in the back, to just below the waist; a black ribbon laced up the back and ended with a big flowing bow over the derriere. It could almost be worn as an evening dress. I went to check the fit and found her in that same position again. Adjusting her necklace and then hands on hips, feet planted slightly apart. Strong and demanding. She was after something, wanting something to happen. I saw that she was wearing a beautiful diamond ring with a matching wedding band, so it wasn't that. I still wasn't getting any vibes from her that she wanted to talk. She asked whether she should wear a suspender belt; I suggested stay ups as the chemise was so tight that it would be seen and ruin the lines. Even the smallest G-string would show, so she was better without.

I chose some eight-denier black stay ups with a red satin top which she was pleased with. She paid for her purchases and left; I was none the wiser as to what her mission was, but there was definitely something going on.

After about a month she returned again. Her red aura was lava-like, but cooling on the edges and outlined in black. She asked again for something special, but this time there was an air of desperation to her request.

"It's got to give me power," she said. "It HAS to work."

I found her a black lace G-sting all in one with an inbuilt sheer lace bra providing fabulous lift. This style always reminded me of Sophia Loren doing her striptease in *Yesterday, Today and Tomorrow*. So very sexy and sophisticated. She tried it on, but this time when I went to check the size, she had abandoned the "strong" stance and was slowly pirouetting in front of the mirror to check the fit and look from every angle.

"If you want to make that look really sexy, why not thread your crucifix through a black velvet ribbon and tie it at your throat?" I suggested. I had also brought in a full-length black chiffon robe with velvet trim and velvet tie to complete the look and a beautiful pair of stay ups that had a line of diamantes instead of a seam up the back of the leg. She was pleased with this look, and as she changed back into her clothes I returned to my desk to wrap them and add up her total.

As she was finding her credit card to pay, she looked me directly in the eyes and finally explained what she was hoping to happen.

"You see—I've become a Christian. I believe that Jesus Christ is my saviour and when I die, I'm going to heaven to sit at his feet. My husband doesn't believe in Jesus or God or anything. As far as I'm concerned that means he's a heathen and when he dies, he's going straight to hell. I can't bear to be without him, so I've been trying to convince him any way I can. I've begged, I've cajoled, I've threatened, I've prayed, I've used my body … but if this doesn't work, I WILL leave him. This is my last shot."

She left, clutching her purchase to her chest and looking so very sad. Her aura had disappeared.

Silver grey

It was a Sunday when he first visited my shop. Tall, lean and in his late teens, he was dressed completely in black: jeans, T-shirt, and a hoodie covering his head. He didn't want to be seen. Avoiding any sort of eye contact with me, he asked if he could look around. He looked so young and was obviously frightened and embarrassed that someone might have seen him walk into a ladies' underwear store.

I left him to browse. He walked around the racks with his head lowered and his hands pushed firmly in his pockets.

He circled all the racks, careful not to touch anything, and then murmured a quiet "Thank you" and left.

Two Sundays later he was back, hoodie in place—but this time when he walked in, he looked me in the eyes and nodded at me. I smiled back and quietly let him know that if he needed any help just to ask. He walked around the racks again but lingered a little longer in front of the nighties. His hands remained firmly in his pockets. He didn't ask for help, so I just let him be. He was so obviously painfully shy, but this time when he left, after about ten minutes, he made eye contact again, nodded and almost smiled as he said "thanks" and left.

A couple of weeks later he was back, but this time when he walked in, he lowered his hoodie. He was obviously starting to feel more comfortable in my presence. He had dark curly hair that hung in soft ringlets to his shoulders. His skin was smooth but there was a bit of growth on his upper lip. He was quite handsome, with high cheekbones and bright blue eyes, but there was a sadness to him that I couldn't quite explain. After a few minutes, he went back to standing in front of the nighties again, so I walked over and asked if he needed any help with sizes.

"I just broke up with my girlfriend three days ago," he explained, his voice soft. "She cheated on me with my best friend. We were together for three years."

"Oh! I'm so sorry," I said. No wonder he looked so sad.

"I'm not. I'm obviously better off without her if she's a cheater." He nodded his head as he spoke, trying to convince himself. He continued quietly, "There is a positive to this, though". He was very well spoken and gentle in his manner, but was quick to point out that while he only liked girls "that way" and was not interested in guys at all, there was something that had become an obsession. He'd always wanted to wear women's underwear. He didn't understand why, couldn't explain it at all, but it was all he could think about. It had nothing to do with sex, he assured me—he just wanted to feel the soft fabrics against his skin.

He looked at me pleadingly, hoping that I would accept him.

He had tried another lingerie store but was chased out with a broom, which made him feel like some kind of deviant. But this was something he felt compelled to explore, so he moved away from his parents, whom he knew would never understand, and into a place of his own. And now, with no girlfriend to worry about, he could wear what he wanted and no one had to know.

He told me his name was Dylan. After the singer, not the poet.

"It's a pleasure to meet you," I told him. "I'm Pauline. Now I'm going to tell you something, and I don't want you to take offence in any way because there is none intended. None at all. It's just that there was a very unfortunate incident here in the past to do with a man trying on things. Let's just say that it ended up with lots of embarrassment for my mum and lots of cleaning fluids."

He looked stricken and horrified.

"Now, I'm not under any circumstances saying that you would do anything like that," I said quickly. "There's a way I can help you. But just so you understand—you'll be the first man in over thirty years that I'll let try anything on. I'm trusting you, just like you trusted me enough to share your secret. However, you can't try on in the change rooms."

He raised an eyebrow—obviously wondering where he was supposed to change but looked clearly relieved that I wasn't refusing him permission

"I have no objections at all, but if a lady customer comes in, she may not understand. Sometimes mums come in with young children as well and it might be more than they are prepared to explain. So, if you wouldn't mind going out the back to the storeroom, there's a bathroom you can use. There's only a head mirror, but it's something at least. Now, why don't you tell me what you would like to try on and I'll find you the right size."

He looked so grateful, and for the first time, he actually pulled his hands out of his pockets to rummage through the rack. He chose a bright blue, floral, knee-length nightie made in a soft jersey and a short green satin nightie with a layer of black lace over the bust. Just then, a couple of ladies walked in, so I winked at him and made a big show of asking if he thought his girlfriend would like them.

"Yes," he replied, looking relieved. "I think she'll like them very much."

I went to help the other ladies, who were just inquiring about the price of a necklace in the window, and after a couple of minutes they left.

I led Dylan to the back room and showed him where the bathroom was. I asked him if he wanted me to check the size; he said yes, and I left him to change. After a few minutes, I heard him call my name and went to see how he was doing. He was standing at the door of the storeroom, looking at me inquisitively as he smoothed down the satin of the green nightie. He had very straight shoulders and narrow hips and absolutely no chest hair. The nightie hung quite well and the lace over the bust disguised the fact that he had no bust to fill it. I told him I would push the mirror that sat at the front of the shop over so he could see how he looked.

Just then a lady walked in; Dylan ran to the bathroom in the back, afraid of being seen. I helped the lady with a pair of stockings and then went to tell Dylan that the coast was clear, so to speak. I found him standing just to the side with his head leaning forward—desperate not to be seen but also desperate to see his reflection. He looked like a cornered and frightened rabbit, not knowing whether it was safer to stand his ground or to run and hide. Terrified, yet so very anxious to see his reflection wearing lingerie for the first-time. It was one of the saddest things I had ever seen.

I pulled the mirror closer. He stepped in front of it and stood and stared at his reflection. His face showed little emotion, but he turned and twisted so he could see himself from every angle. His aura began to change from grey to silver as his lips curled into a smile and his eyes lit up. "I'm going to try on the other one now if that's all right," he said, heading back to the bathroom to change. A few minutes later, he reappeared in the blue floral jersey, which just needed adjusting on the straps. I thought it was too loose over his narrow hips, but he liked it, so I left him to admire his reflection in the mirror.

After about ten minutes, he came out all smiles and said he wanted both of them. I wrapped them for him; as he left, he thanked me, placed his hoodie back over his head and beat a quick escape.

Dylan has been coming in every six months or so for the last five years. He no longer covers his head as he walks in, and he knows his way to the back room without asking. He has had some breast forms made—he wanted to get DDs, but I talked him into a generous C cup instead, as it would look more in proportion with his narrow frame. He's still a SILVER/GREY, but now his aura is definitely sparkling. Like Diamonds. He has had a number of girlfriends over the years, but no-one he trusts enough to share his secret with.

Yet.

For more Secret Women's Business visit:

www.secretwomensbusinesslingerie.com

Or visit the shop:

Secret Women's Business Lingerie

91 Willoughby Rd

Crows Nest 2065

New South Wales